Creative Gremlins

Write your way through
doubt and fear to claim
your creative life

NICOLA JACKSON & TERESA WILSON

THE
Unstoppable
Author

To Mary and Terry Wilson

Seven Creative Gremlins

CONTENTS

Introduction

MEET YOUR CREATIVE GREMLINS

Wondering why you're having difficulty starting, sticking with or completing a writing project?

Meet your **Creative Gremlins**. It seems to be a law of nature that every time a person embarks on a piece of creative work – whether for the first time or the fiftieth – then these mischievous creatures come along for the ride.

The Gremlins come in many shapes, sizes, and disguises, but they all have one aim in common: to knock your confidence, belittle and attack you, and generally ensure that you abandon your creative project.

Creative Gremlins are the reason so many people long to write but never set down a single word. They're why some of those who *do* dare to commit their ideas to the page quickly stop, put their work away and never touch it again.

They're the reason you might have started twenty projects and finished none of them. They are why even 'successful' writers sometimes fear to begin their next story.

But it's okay to have these Gremlins. In fact, it's perfectly normal. The truth is, there's just no way to get on the creative road without the Gremlins showing up. They come with the territory, as integral to your journey as a Sat Nav and a packet of boiled sweets. By learning to understand and eventually circumvent these troublemakers, you'll also be learning how to strengthen your creativity, develop a habit of tenacity, and nurture a self-belief, determination and commitment to your craft that you wouldn't otherwise have had access to.

Ultimately, our **Creative Gremlins** strengthen us as creative people. It's just *they* don't know that.

TRAVELLING WITH GREMLINS
So, let's go on a road trip.

Along the way, you're going to meet the seven most common **Creative Gremlins**. The ones most likely to show up and attempt to sabotage your journey. We'll share ideas on how you can keep them quiet, distract them, or kick them to the curb completely, allowing you to start, stick with and reach *the end* of your creative projects.

YOUR MILEAGE MAY VARY
What we're sharing in this book is the product of decades spent working with our own creativity and also of working with, and alongside, other artists as friends, colleagues and coaches. These

are the challenges that we have experienced most frequently and the workarounds that we've found to be most effective.

But we also know that everyone's creative path and process is individual. If you find certain sections speak to you, that's fantastic. If you find yourself baulking against some of the suggestions we make, that's great too. It's all good information. Reacting against an idea or a piece of advice tells you as much about your own creative process as would wholeheartedly agreeing with us.

We're not interested in dictating a prescribed path through creativity (there is no such thing, anyway). Our goal is to help you to strengthen your creative muscles and your artistic instincts so that you can forge your own way with excitement and confidence; reclaiming your creativity and enriching your life.

On board with that? Fabulous. Then on we go.

WHY GREMLINS DO WHAT THEY DO

As we've mentioned, **Creative Gremlins** have only one aim in mind: they want to derail your creative ventures. But why?

The inner workings of our Gremlins will be broken down in each chapter, but the overall motivation of a Gremlin is quite simple and actually pretty benevolent: they think they're helping you.

Creativity is an amazing process; one that stretches us as human beings like nothing else can. It causes us to experience some incredible things: growth, joy, fun, mastery, bliss. But it also demands that we encounter some things that are very challenging and uncomfortable. These include change, risk, uncertainty, rejection and failure.

Now, the latter all seem a bit too frightening for a Gremlin. Although they might act tough, deep down your **Creative Gremlins** are timid and fearful beasts. They don't like risk, they don't like change, they *certainly* don't like rejection. And because where you go, they go, if you embark on a creative path, they have no choice but to come along and experience all of the above with you.

"No thank you," your Gremlins say. "It's a hard pass from us!"

That's why they'll do absolutely anything they can to stop you from writing. We don't blame them. We understand that your Gremlins think creativity is a Very Bad Thing.

We just happen to know they're wrong.

WHAT YOU'LL NEED FOR THIS ROAD TRIP

While you can read this book and learn theoretically about the most common **Creative Gremlins**, you'll get far more from the process if you make it a practical learning experience.

What this means is that we're asking you to begin a writing project. It doesn't matter what it is – it could be a short story, a novel, a piece of non-fiction, an article, a poem or a review. It could be a brand-new piece of work or something you've started but haven't finished. All that matters is that it's something you're excited about – a journey that you really want to go on.

Begin your creative project alongside reading this book and you won't just learn about the Gremlins; you'll meet them face to face. This is hugely beneficial. It will show you how these purveyors of creative doubt and fear show up in your particular case. This offers you an invaluable practical guide to your own writing process, to the obstacles you're most likely to face, and to the best ways to navigate past them.

Got a project in mind for this writing road trip?

Wonderful. Then let's begin.

CHAPTER ONE

The Imposter Syndrome Gremlin who says:

"You're not a writer."

1

PREPARING FOR YOUR CREATIVE JOURNEY

So, you're ready for your creative road trip. You've got an idea that you're really excited about and you're starting to think about getting your ideas down on paper. There's no harm in having a go, right? And you don't actually have to tell anyone you're doing it.

What could possibly go wrong?

Right on cue, up stomps our **Imposter Syndrome Gremlin**. With an incredulous look on its face, it blocks our way, bellowing, "Write something? You? HA! Are you kidding me? You're not a writer!"

This is our first Gremlin and this blunt individual frequently stops us from ever even beginning. This creature bars the way to your creative road trip and is the reason many people who long to write have never dared to put pen to paper.

The **Imposter Syndrome Gremlin** often targets new writers; those who have been eyeing up a creative pursuit for many years but haven't yet had the courage to do anything about it. Such writers, being inexperienced, are very vulnerable to this Gremlin's harshly negative schtick.

The **Imposter Syndrome Gremlin** can be so hurtful and so convincing that after hearing its merciless judgement, many aspiring writers immediately put their creative projects away for good, suffering a scalding sense of shame that they ever had the audacity to think they could be a writer in the first place!

But, then again, **Imposter** is an equal opportunities beast. It'll target experienced writers, too, pointing out, "Sure, you managed to fool them last time, but this time everyone's going to realise that you don't belong. Yeah, start that writing project but, just so you know, you're wasting your time. In fact, you know what? Stop embarrassing yourself by trying to be a writer because everyone knows you're a fake."

Brutal. But then, **Creative Gremlins** are brutal. Their one job is to stop you from taking risks or trying. **Imposter Syndrome Gremlin** can show up anywhere; for example, if you start a new job or become a parent for the first time. But in those circumstances, you have to dig deep and work through the discomfort. You can't send that baby back, after all! But with your creativity? If it hurts? Well, if no one is standing over you, waiting for your creative output, then it's much easier for the **Imposter Syndrome Gremlin** to convince you to stop, often before you've even started.

THAT SINKING FEELING
You'll know if you've encountered the **Imposter Syndrome Gremlin** because even thinking about starting to write will make

you uncomfortable. You might have kept your aspirations secret because you feel weird and embarrassed about admitting to them, and so this makes it even easier to quit, since no one knew you were trying to write in the first place. Or maybe you've had a break from creativity and are planning to get back to it but somehow you just can't quite bring yourself to make a start.

If you've encountered this Gremlin, you might even have convinced yourself that writing and creativity isn't your path. That other people get to be artists, but not you. In fact, you've changed your mind; you don't want to be a writer after all! Eventually, you'll have repeated this often enough to yourself that you start to believe it.

And so, thanks to the **Imposter Syndrome Gremlin**, yet another story remains untold, yet another poem never sees the light of day, yet another creative soul finds themselves cut off from their spark, and perhaps grows a little sadder, a little more lost to themselves, a little more unfulfilled without really understanding why. Another wonderful and exhilarating creative journey is called off before it has even begun.

WHY THE IMPOSTER SYNDROME GREMLIN IS SO PERSUASIVE

Okay, so now we are aware that, just as we pick up the car keys and look like we're about to embark on our creative trip, this Gremlin is very likely to turn up and declare that we're simply not up to the challenge.

But why are we so eager to believe it?

Let's dig a little deeper into the effectiveness of this Gremlin.

There are two parts to this. The first is what you believe a *writer* to be. The second is what you believe *yourself* to be.

> *"If you find yourself asking yourself (and your friends), "Am I really a writer? Am I really an artist?" chances are you are. The counterfeit innovator is wildly self-confident. The real one is scared to death."*
> Steven Pressfield, *The War of Art* (2012)[i]

WHAT IS A WRITER, ANYWAY?

Let's start with your definition of a writer. What comes to mind when you think of a writer?

Is it someone accomplished and at the top of their game? Someone recognised and respected by the literary press? Someone validated by their success and making huge amounts of money from their work? Or do you have a picture of the fabled starving artist? Someone who has shunned the comforts of the world to passionately and single-mindedly focus on their art? A genius in a garret, obsessive and brilliant but with a terrible personal life and a deepening alcohol problem?

And yet, let's just have a quick look at the definition of a writer, as according to the Oxford English Dictionary.

Firstly, here's the definition that many aspiring writers fixate on. A writer is, "A person who writes books, stories, or articles as a job or occupation." And, if you aren't doing it as a job or getting paid for it? Well, how can you call yourself a writer?

But wait a minute, the OED also says a writer is: "A person who has written something or who writes in a particular way."

Hmm. So, actually, as far as the OED is concerned, if you have written *something*, then you are a writer. (We all write in a particular way, so that one's a given.) Notice that, in this definition, the OED doesn't mention anything about how famous you have to be, how much work you have to have completed, how respected you are, or how much you've suffered for your art. All it says is that you have to *have written something*.

The key, it seems, is taking action.

This is why the **Imposter Syndrome Gremlin** is always the first to strike.

Just when you were about to embark on the act that would make you feel like a writer, it tells you that you're not one and so shames you into stopping!

The wonderful thing is, if you can learn to ignore the Gremlin and make a start on your creative project, the very minute you pick up a pen or open a new blank document on your computer and start to write, you become a writer – because you have written something. Maybe not a complete something, but definitely a something.

Now, listen, we get it. Calling yourself a writer can feel very exposing so we're not telling you to have it embossed on a T-shirt, get it put on your passport or announce it to strangers as your calling in life – unless you want to, in which case; go for it! But what we are saying is that you could experiment with *thinking of yourself as a writer* – i.e., someone who writes.

Because the truth is, you cannot wait to 'feel like a writer' before you begin. It is the beginning to write that *turns* you into a writer.

WHO AM I, ANYWAY?

Of course, even knowing all of that, it's not always as simple as, "just ignore the Gremlin." As well as having to tell yourself a new, more accurate story about what being a writer means, you'll also have to unpick the story you've been telling yourself about *who you are*.

And the chances are, if you are vulnerable to the **Imposter Syndrome Gremlin**, you might have formulated an idea about yourself that contradicts the idea of being 'a writer.'

How might this happen? Well, our sense of self is a complex thing. We start to construct our identities in childhood and, since this is a rather weighty job for someone who can't even master two plus two yet, it's no wonder that sometimes our sense of self turns out a bit wonky.

Let's start at the beginning. When you were born, you looked to your caregivers to meet your basic needs – food, comfort, protection, safety.

As you got older, you came to understand that you were a separate being from your primary caregiver and therefore had to begin to develop an individual sense of self. After all, if you're not them, who are you?

And so, you looked around, antennae tuned, hoovering up any information that would help you make sense of your place in the world. The only trouble is, our child brains took in information and rendered it fact.

You may have had an experience at school that taught you, "I have to be quiet to be approved of." You might have failed a spelling test and concluded, "I'm no good at English." A bad experience on the football pitch might lead you to the certainty, "I'm rubbish at sport." A grown-up's adverse reaction to a childhood upset might leave you with the belief, "It's not ok to show my emotions."

We keep on collecting these 'facts' about ourselves; slotting them into our sense of identity as though they're true.

"I'm a good girl."

"People won't like me if I show off."

"I'm clumsy."

"I'm stupid."

"I'm no good with money."

And so on, and so on.

These flawed beliefs are like pictures in an art gallery, which we believe represent us. But as we grow older, rather than constantly updating our pictures to reflect a more accurate sense of ourselves, we often go through life unconsciously looking for and collecting more examples that reaffirm these false beliefs, these distorted pictures, even if it's illogical:

"I didn't get that job. It's because I'm stupid."

"John dumped me. It's because I'm stupid."

"I missed the bus. It's because I'm stupid."

I TOLD YOU: I'M NOT A WRITER

What does this have to do with calling yourself a writer? Well, if the thought of describing yourself as one makes you feel uncomfortable, then it's likely that somewhere along the line you have created a limiting belief around it.

At some point in your life, you'll have developed a belief about yourself, others, or the world that clashes with the notion, "I am a writer." This means that, when you start to think it, you activate an earlier, contradictory thought and it makes you feel bad.

The earlier thought could be something like: "I'm not an imaginative person." Or: "If I express myself, people will laugh." Or: "I shouldn't show off." Or: "People from backgrounds like mine don't do things like that."

It doesn't have to be something that someone has said to you. It can simply be an experience from which you formed a limiting belief.

> *"When I started the research on shame, you know, 13 years ago, I found that 85% of the men and women who I interviewed remembered an event in school that was so shaming, it changed how they thought of themselves for the rest of their lives. But wait – this is good – 50% of that 85%, half of those people: those shame wounds were around creativity. So 50% of those people have art scars. Have creativity scars."*
>
> Brené Brown on "Big Strong Magic"', (2016) Elizabeth Gilbert: 'Magic Lessons' Podcast)[ii]

Something inside you is pulling you to writing (we know this is true because you are reading this book). But another something is saying that you absolutely can't – and that it has the evidence to prove it.

Our brains *can* hold both of these ideas at the same time, but there'll be discomfort.

And, as our brains like to use the least amount of energy possible and discomfort means expending energy, they prefer running old 'maps of the world' rather than investing the effort in creating new ones. This means that the brain will quickly find evidence to back up the earlier thought so that it can dismiss the new one:

> "Remember when you were nine and brought that drawing home and mum put it in the bin? And when you wore those leg warmers to school, and everyone laughed? And that perm…that didn't go well either, did it? The evidence clearly shows that expressing yourself is bad, so it's a *no* to you being a writer, I'm afraid. It's just not safe."

Can you see how the **Imposter Syndrome Gremlin** can be so damn persuasive? Many of us are already primed *not* to believe we are writers or artists. And if thinking we might be one makes us feel very uncomfortable and at risk of ridicule or shame, of course we'll be predisposed to accept what this bullying Gremlin tells us.

The good news is that we're not stuck with these limiting beliefs. The 'facts' we took on board when we were young are not set in stone. They can be updated. And they should be.

It's time for us to refresh our internal art gallery; to hang a few gorgeous new pictures on the walls that better represent who we are now.

So, how do we go about doing this?

GETTING PAST THE IMPOSTER SYNDROME GREMLIN

A powerful thing to do at this stage of your creative journey is to simply notice what is coming up for you.

When you think about starting your writing project, you might not initially notice the **Imposter Syndrome Gremlin** whispering in your ear. You might think *its* thoughts are your thoughts and find it difficult to tell the difference between them at first.

One trick to help you tune in more closely is to notice what you feel in your body when you begin to think about writing. Physiological reactions are clues to what's going on in your mind. If you feel a bit funny or tense, you're probably thinking a thought that challenges an earlier thought. You've started to think of yourself as a writer and your **Imposter Syndrome Gremlin** has popped up to save you from yourself. That's fine. It just means you're on the right track.

Changing our limiting beliefs is a process that doesn't happen overnight. But starting to become more aware of them can be a powerful step to begin the process. As you start to examine your thoughts more closely, you may find that some belong to **Imposter Syndrome Gremlin** – and these are the ones you can choose to challenge over time.

CHANGING YOUR MINDSET

You can also do some warm-up exercises to help bring you into a positive mindset; a state of allowing and awareness that will encourage you to begin. Taking action is a powerful way of overriding the limiting effect of an out-of-date belief and, as we said before, once you are *doing*, you're automatically a writer!

1. Act as if

Does it serve you to hold the belief, 'I am not a writer'? Does it help you create? If not, then switch the thought and act 'as if', even if you don't believe the new thought yet.

Just say it, think it, own it. Stick it on a Post-it on your bathroom mirror: "I am a writer." (Because, why *not* believe it?!)

Then practice bringing this thought into your everyday life. For instance, let's say you wrote something for work that you were proud of and one of your colleagues admired it, but you catch yourself thinking, "It was just work. My colleague was probably just being polite. It was nothing special."

Ah! Is that the **Imposter Syndrome Gremlin** we hear? Every time you do something even *slightly* creative and then catch yourself feeling this sense of defeatism or disapproval, just switch your mindset and tell yourself, "I *am* a writer!"

You don't have to *believe* it immediately, but just get used to countering your Gremlin as this will help you to understand that *its* voice is not *your* voice. After all, it's only once you understand your opponent, that you can challenge and change it.

As Amy Cuddy says in her great TED Talk on the subject, "Don't fake it till you make it. Fake it till you become it. Do it enough until you actually become it and internalize it."[iii]

As we say; you're a writer. If anyone can change the story you're telling yourself, it is you!

2. Journalling

Journalling – pouring out a stream of consciousness onto the page, without censoring or judgement – is an incredible resource for anyone who wants to clear some space in their brains for the good stuff to appear. It can also support you in understanding more about yourself.

Developing self-awareness is a key component in your journey to becoming a writer. *You* are the key asset in your creative toolbox. Everything that you create will be unique and incredible because it will be what *only* you can make. So the more you connect with yourself, the more you understand yourself, the more fulfilling your creative process will feel.

Now, let's be clear: journalling is not about penning rich prose and stunning philosophical insights that will be published after you're dead. It's about getting rid of the junk in our heads. Therefore, what we write down usually consists of head-vomit – a stream of consciousness and nonsensical mundanity. Disposable as product, but golden as process. Nobody is going to read it and you don't even have to read it back yourself. The value is in the doing.

By developing the habit of regular journaling – of getting words down on the page without censure or self-criticism – we strengthen our connection to our creativity and begin to reclaim the artist inside us. We realise that being a creative person does not require anyone's permission. All it requires is action. The only way through is to start. We recommend committing to a daily practice or, if that's too much initially, writing for at least ten minutes before any writing session you have planned.

And eventually, the next time your **Imposter Syndrome Gremlin** stands there, arms folded, scoffing, "What do you think you're doing? You're not a writer!" you can simply shrug and say, "Well, I'm writing, aren't I?"

We hope that by the end of this chapter, you'll have a) wrapped your head around the idea of calling yourself a writer, and b) begun to understand that the **Imposter Syndrome Gremlin** is simply operating on old beliefs to try to save you from your exciting but challenging adventure.

So, are you ready to call yourself a writer?

Great, because it's time to start our creative journey. And it's in making a start on writing that we meet the next of our charming little friends.

CHAPTER ONE QUICK MAP

- You may be intimidated, embarrassed or afraid to call yourself 'a writer'

- You may have fixed notions of what it means to be a writer that conflict with your ideas of yourself

- In fact, a writer is just someone who has written something, so once you start, you are one!

- With awareness and persistence, it is entirely possible to update your map of the world to include the belief, 'I am a writer'

HOW AUTHORS BECOME UNSTOPPABLE #1
Maria Roberts, author of Single Mother on the Verge (Penguin)

When I first started writing I had a small child. I was in my early twenties and had an insane amount of enthusiasm and energy and (looking back) fewer worries than in my forties, simply because you don't sweat the small stuff in your twenties, whereas, as I passed through my thirties and into my forties, I became more cautious and responsible. In my twenties, I would write when my son had gone to bed, while waiting in the playground on the school run, in cafés, even on New Year's Eve and Christmas Day. Writing wasn't something I had to do but something special I looked forward to doing.

A few years after Single Mother on the Verge was published I went through a long stretch of really needing to earn a decent salary - teenagers are expensive. I also wanted to travel and try new things. I became the editor of an international arts magazine and was lucky enough to travel to places as far ranging as New York, Yerevan, Riga and Oslo to name a few. I stopped living at my desk and I saw the world

I'm 41 now and going back to writing. I think 'writing' and 'not writing' is like being fit and unfit – you know you can get there, but you have to build up your stamina. I'm getting back into the swing of things by going to talks, galleries, watching films, reading books, exploring new places and being alone to think. My son has moved into student digs now so I don't have any excuses.

My advice to other writers is don't ever stop. I am getting back into my stride by reading work at events again, hearing people laugh makes me really happy. When I'm in a fug of nerves, I try to recapture the blind optimism of my twenties by looking at old photos. Having a strong and determined friendship group helps; being competitive is no bad thing. Try not to be too focused on the outcome. It may sound like a cliché but the truth is that you have to create because you enjoy it – if that joy is missing, the dullness will come through in your writing. So finding joy in what you do is important. In the face of rejection or setbacks remind yourself that this is your thing, your pride and joy, and not theirs.

CHAPTER TWO

The Control Freak Gremlin who says:

"You can't start until you're absolutely ready."

BEGINNING YOUR CREATIVE JOURNEY

So, you've just about got your head around calling yourself a writer. You're ready to experience uncomfortable feelings due to past experiences and limiting beliefs, because you know you can rewrite those 'facts' which no longer accurately represent you as a person.

You also know that the only way to be a writer is to dive in and start writing. You're excited to get started. Hooray!

Except, also, boo! Because just when we're ready to begin, that's when we encounter our next little annoyance; the **Control Freak Gremlin.**

This Gremlin is sneaky. It can see that you're all set to go. You've filled the tank, you've got the car keys in your hand, the driving gloves are on, you're ready to roll!

That's when this Gremlin rushes up to us, shrieking, "I just hope you know where you are going! You don't want to get lost! It's so scary and dangerous out there…"

And just like that, we doubt ourselves again.

Because, no, we don't know where we're going. No, we're not sure what's going to happen. We don't know exactly what we're going to write in this session we've made time for. And we were about to do it anyway! Yikes!

What the hell were we thinking?

Again, this is a Gremlin that really likes to get its claws into new writers, who often aren't yet sure how this whole creative thing works. The **Control Freak Gremlin** knows that it can easily persuade them that all other writers in the world are confident, certain and assured before they put pen to paper or fingertips to keyboard. (A complete lie, but a convincing one.) It plants the worry that you can't start until you really know what you're doing.

This Gremlin's only job is to make you believe you're not ready yet, but (crucially) that you could be if you just prepared a little more.

And why? Because if it can convince you that you need to plan your creative route minutely and exactly ahead of time, making sure you have all the right equipment and are deeply knowledgeable about anything and everything that might happen along the way…well, chances are you'll spend so long trying to be 'ready', you'll never actually set off.

"Writing is like driving at night in the fog. You can only see as far as your headlights, but you can make the whole trip that way."
E. L. Doctorow

PLANNING THE UNPLANNABLE

You'll know if you've encountered this Gremlin if every time you think about doing some writing, you suddenly realise that there's a huge amount of preparation required before you can start.

When this Gremlin hits, instead of writing we make a deal with ourselves. Okay, we say, we definitely *will* start writing, just as soon as we have a brilliant idea. Just as soon as we know where the brilliant idea is going. Just as soon as we feel we can do justice to that brilliant idea we've planned out!

But do we know when that time is? When we feel like we know exactly what we are doing on our creative journey and feel supremely confident in setting off?

That's right. Never.

Of course, the **Control Freak Gremlin** knows this full well. This panic-stricken saboteur is fully aware that, very often, embarking on a creative project involves setting off with only the vaguest idea of where you're heading and just blind faith that you'll get there.

And this Gremlin's fear is infectious. "Oh my God," you think. "I can't believe I was going to start writing when I've no idea what

I'm doing! I'm clueless! Who am I fooling? I just need to do some more preparation..." And so, instead of making a start on your writing road trip, you pore over the map. You plot and replot the route. You wax the car and triple-check the oil and…well, there goes your writing road trip time.

And all the while, the **Control Freak Gremlin** is breathing a sigh of relief because it knows something that you don't know, yet: that there's no way to be truly 'ready'.

Again, the **Control Freak Gremlin** is not above tormenting experienced writers with its neurosis, either.

"Okay," it'll say, "that story you wrote last time turned out fine but now you need to live up to those expectations. What, you're going to risk just launching yourself into writing and hope for the best? Don't be ridiculous. People expect good stuff from you now. You have deadlines! You need to get serious about this. You need to plan and prepare and make damn certain that you create something really special."

And so instead of getting down to writing, you find yourself sharpening all of your HB pencils down to the nib. And then going out to buy new ones.

> *"I write to discover what I know."*
> Flannery O'Connor

WHY THE CONTROL FREAK GREMLIN IS SO PERSUASIVE

So, we understand that this Gremlin will attempt to undermine us and make us believe that we're simply not equipped to make this journey. That setting off unprepared is deeply unsafe.

But why does it work so effectively?

To answer this, we need to look at how we have been conditioned to behave in our everyday adult lives.

Creativity is the act of making something out of nothing. Often, there's no five-point plan. No agenda. No certainty. No mastery. At least, not at this stage. Even writers who like to plot their books out in great detail will be conscious that they must be flexible with those limitations and restrictions to get the best results.

We believe that true creativity utilises more of us than just our brains. We think that the subconscious loves to get stuck in, too, which means we have to trust that even when we don't consciously know what we are doing, somehow there is a sort of knowing going on. A kind of plan. Just one we are not yet aware of and can't control.

In our experience, creativity is at its best and most thrilling when we're just stumbling in the dark, working everything out as we go. This is a free and almost childlike state of pure creative inspiration and invention.

The problem is, most of us have been avoiding this state of free-fall cluelessness for a very long time. As adults, we're supposed to know what we're doing. As employees, as bill-payers, as parents, as responsible citizens, we have to be competent. I mean, you can hardly turn up to work and say to your boss, "Today's board meeting? Oh, I thought I'd just start talking and see what happens!"

We've spent years practising being sure about things and now creativity is asking us to just give a metaphorical shrug and say, "I dunno!"

THE ART OF FEELING LOST

Not knowing what you're doing can feel terrible at first, prompting a great amount of self-criticism and even shame. This can be devastating if you're not expecting it but begins to feel more comfortable once you realise that the ability to tolerate the feeling is an integral part of the creative process.

It doesn't matter how long ago you were in contact with that free, childlike, creative self; they are still inside you, just waiting for you to give them some time to emerge.

For many of us, it has been a while since we've experienced that state and felt that kind of exhilarating freedom. But here's the amazing flip side to there being no 'correct' instructions for your creativity: this is *your* creative project.

There's no boss peering over your shoulder.

You're not getting an appraisal on this. And there's no way to get it wrong. You say what goes, and so you can give yourself permission to not know what the hell you are doing, but to go ahead and do it anyway.

THE INSPIRATION GAME

Another sneaky way the **Control Freak Gremlin** will attempt to get to you is by telling you, "Well, okay, so maybe you don't need that special writer's desk, or that expensive writer's software, or that jaunty writer's hat I had my eye on for you, but you at least have to wait for inspiration to strike."

We respectfully disagree.

In our experience, ideas will begin to emerge while you are in the act of doing. Inspiration and creativity don't tend to visit when we are standing still, tapping our watch and waiting. They seem to like to meet us when we are already in motion. (Or in the shower, but that's a whole other subject.)

I'M JUST NOT FEELING IT

But you can only start writing when you're feeling really gung-ho and enthusiastic about it, right?

Again, *no*.

Creativity is amazing. It makes us feel good, it connects us to ourselves, it gets us into a state of flow, and it gives us a feeling that nothing else can duplicate. But are you always going to feel like doing it? Erm…nope.

Why not, if it feels so good? Doesn't that mean you're not really a writer after all? (Oh look, there's the **Imposter Syndrome Gremlin** again. These creatures do not respect boundaries. They'll take any opportunity to reappear if they spot that you're having a moment of doubt!)

Okay, here's the thing. We believe that creativity is a bit like exercise or meditation.

It feels amazing when you're doing it, you're always thankful you bothered, the health rewards are wonderful, and yet…the next time class rolls around, isn't there often a teensy bit of resistance to going? Even though you know you'll enjoy it when you get there?

Absolutely there is. (Hence the legions of unused gym memberships and very dusty yoga mats.)

Well, creativity feels like this too. We know it's great. We definitely want to do it. But if we always waited until we felt massively enthused about getting stuck in? Well let's just say there are plenty of incredible novels that would have remained unwritten.

I DON'T HAVE THE TIME TO WRITE

We're not going to argue that your life isn't busy. Modern life is filled with demands, obligations and untold distractions. But there are writers who are publishing work while working a full-time job, looking after sick relatives and raising kids. There are others who have a quiet, relatively undemanding life who somehow only manage a few hundred words every other month. And there's everything else in between.

When you decide to write, you can't wait for the point at which you feel you have the time. That's just the **Control Freak Gremlin**'s way of making you put off your creativity indefinitely.

Just like you might never feel uber-confident about setting pen to paper, you might go a decade without getting that gap in the schedule in which you believe you can write your masterpiece. (Have you ever noticed that just when you think you've taken care of all your 'life stuff', you look around and there's just another pile of stuff waiting for your attention?)

There *is* time for writing in your life. We know there is.

Right now, you may be spending that time on family and friends, on TV, on shopping, on cleaning your house, or browsing social media. But if you're serious about writing, you're going to need to bump creativity up your list of priorities. And – we cannot stress this enough – take time to be offline. The internet sucks up your time while giving very little in return, except for worry, annoyance, and 'comparison-itis' – and is rapidly becoming one of the main reasons that writers don't do any actual writing.

PLOTTING AND PANTSING

A quick side note on planning when it comes to stories. Some people are 'plotters' – they like to have the next scene, the next chapter or the entire story/book planned out before they make a start. Some famous plotters include J.K. Rowling and John Grisham.

Some people are what's known in the writing community as 'pantsers' (because they fly by the seat of their pants). These writers don't know where their story is going to take them, and they don't want to. They just follow their intuition, go where their creativity takes them and eventually end up with a completed story.

Some famous pantsers are Stephen King and Margaret Atwood.

Just as with everything in writing, there are extreme plotters and extreme pantsers and everything else in between. Some people plot a dozen chapters ahead but are happy for their story to take a diversion if that's where it wants to go.

Some writers will perfect every sentence before they move onto the next. Some orchestrate every twist. Some are as surprised by their twist as the reader eventually will be. There is no right or wrong way, there's just your way – the way that gets your story out into the world to the best of your ability.

But hang on! This is not an excuse to spend months and years outlining your novel because you've decided you're a plotter, because, guess what? You can't find out where you fit on the plotter-pantser continuum until you've actually done some writing! Got it? Great, now back to that pesky Gremlin…

GETTING PAST THE CONTROL FREAK GREMLIN

All of the **Control Freak Gremlin**'s methods aim to make us feel so overwhelmed that we eventually find it's just easier to give up on the whole idea of writing.

But there's one simple way to get around the Gremlin's myriad tricks and that's to set yourself a routine and stick to it.

> *"No one "builds a house." They lay one brick again and again and again and the end result is a house. The average day in a wannabe author's week and a real author's week looks almost the same. The real author writes a couple pages, laying a brick, and the wannabe author writes nothing. 98% of their day is otherwise identical. But a year later, the real author has a completed first draft of a book and the wannabe author has…nothing. It's all about the bricks."*

Tim Urban, www.waitbutwhy.com[iv]

THE MAGIC OF ROUTINE

I know what you're thinking: "Hang on a minute, you just said I can't plan my creativity! Besides, I'm a writer, an artist! Writers don't have schedules and timetables! Shouldn't artists just go with the flow?"

Well, it's true that you can't always plan the 'what', but you can certainly plan the 'when'. And you probably should. Because though it may seem paradoxical, some structure to your writing life can really help free up your creativity.

And here's why:

DECISION MAKING TAKES ENERGY

In *Your Brain at Work* (2009), David Rock writes, "Making decisions relies heavily on a region of the brain called the prefrontal cortex. The prefrontal cortex chews up metabolic fuel, such as glucose and oxygen, faster than people realise.

Dr. Roy Baumeister from Florida University explains, "We have a limited bucket of resources for activities like decision-making and impulse control, and when we use these up we don't have as much for the next activity.""[v]

Your brain has limited capacity. It likes shortcuts. So, if you make a decision once and commit to it, you free up more capacity for your creative endeavour.

SCHEDULING PACIFIES THE CONTROL FREAK GREMLIN

If you're a new writer, you're likely to be vulnerable to the **Control Freak Gremlin**'s anguished cries about how we need to *plan* every single thing!

While this obsession with knowing what's going to happen is not always helpful in the creative sphere, you can put it to use when it comes to organising your time.

Our creative self is rather like a two-year-old: great at slapping paint on a cavass without self-consciousness, but not particularly adept at timetabling.

So why not get your adult self to give your creative self a time slot for writing?

Get your diary and mark out your designated writing time. And then do it.

No questioning, no over-thinking, no decision-making involved. You just do it, because you've been told to do it by your adult self.

PLANNING WRITING SENDS A MESSAGE

By putting that writing session in the calendar, you're also sending an important message to yourself and to the people around you that writing is important to you.

Look around you. I bet there are people in your life who are making damn sure that they get their time to watch sport, go to the gym, or do whatever else it is that makes them *them*.

Well, hold on a minute. You're a writer. Writing makes you *you*. But only you are going to insist that you do it. Because, to be perfectly blunt, no one else cares enough about your creativity to make sure you do this writing. Indeed, as nice as your friends and family no doubt are, they might even prefer it if you *didn't* write, when you could be doing something that contributes more to *their* life and happiness instead. (And also, in some instances, so that you don't start reminding them about their own creative selves that they've long since buried.)

So, don't wait for a cheerleader or a boss to make you do it. No one is coming. You are *it*.

You have to prioritise it. *You* have to care.

LEARN FROM THE GREATS

Still unsure whether scheduling writing time can help your creativity? Well, don't just take it from us…

> *"I keep to this routine every day without variation. The repetition itself becomes the important thing."*
> Haruki Murakami

"I never could have done what I have done without the habits of punctuality, order, and diligence."
Charles Dickens

"Be regular and orderly in your life, so that you may be violent and original in your work."
Gustave Flaubert

"Order and simplification are the first steps toward the mastery of a subject."
Thomas Mann

"The cumulative power of doing things the same way every day seems to be a way of saying to the mind: You're going to be dreaming soon."
Stephen King

HOW TO ROUTINE

What should your routine look like? This is your project, and so the answer to that question is entirely up to you. It might be half an hour daily, an hour weekly, or every other Saturday. You might be a morning lark or a night owl, writing when your kids/partner/friends/the world is sleeping! You might write in bursts for weeks at a time and then do nothing for a month. You may have to experiment for a while until you find the writing routine that brings out the best in you, and that most suits your life and your creative temperament.

Just know that the more you commit to showing up at the page, the more likely it is your creativity will show up too. After all, you've proven yourself to be a reliable partner in this writing business, so why wouldn't it?

And when your **Control Freak Gremlin** starts worrying away at you again, telling you that you don't know what you're doing, you can simply reply, "Sure I do. I'm turning up at 3pm on Friday. So, shush."

The chances are, that'll shut your Gremlin right up.

Okay, so, you've decided you're a writer, you've made a commitment to writing without knowing exactly what you're doing, and you've set off on your journey. You're on the road. Amazing news!

But, uh-oh. Look who's stowed away in the back seat.

CHAPTER TWO QUICK MAP

- It is tempting to wait until you are 'ready'

- You don't have to know what you are doing in order to start

- You can access inspiration and creativity through taking action

- A routine can bypass this Gremlin's many, many reasons not to write

- Your brain likes routine because making decisions takes energy

- The routine you choose is up to you

HOW AUTHORS BECOME UNSTOPPABLE #2
Andrea Mara, author of One Click (Poolbeg Press)

I write in the morning when my kids are at school, and again at night when they're in bed, but I found I was struggling with productivity. I am a plotter - I absolutely have to know what's going to happen in the next chapter, otherwise I either meander all over the place or sit staring at a blank page. But then half my morning was being taken up with plotting, leaving me frustrated about how little time I was actually spending writing. Then at night, I was too tired to write with any great productivity.

So I switched things around – now I always plot at night, so I'm ready to go at 9am the following morning – straight down to writing. I am much better at paper-and-pen plotting at night than I ever was at writing too. The only sad thing is it took me two years to realise I needed to shift things around!
The other thing I've started recently is promising myself a treat at every 10,000 words. If I don't get a chance to hit the shops I double up at the next milestone. It might be a nail varnish or a new dress, but it definitely helps keep me pushing up the word count!

The Hyper-Critical Gremlin who says:

"You're terrible at this! You should quit."

UNDERSTANDING YOUR CREATIVE JOURNEY

By now you'll appreciate that it might feel difficult to call yourself a writer but you're going to call yourself one anyway. You understand that the notion of being completely prepared for all eventualities is just a ruse to prevent you from starting. And you've decided to set off.

Congratulations, you are officially on the road! Whoop whoop! So, there you are, cruising down the creative highway, with your favourite tunes on the radio and the wind in your hair. Feels great, doesn't it? At least at first. But hey, who's this?

Ah. It seems you've got a stowaway on board.

Introducing: The **Hyper-Critical Gremlin**.

This nasty little imp surfaces as soon as you've decided that you're definitely going on your creative journey. Once you've set off, it'll climb out from under its blanket, switch off the radio and confiscate your travel sweets.

That done, the Gremlin will then begin a steady flow of negativity, letting you know that: "You're terrible at this. Really, truly terrible. You should give up now."

The **Hyper-Critical Gremlin** never gets bored of criticising. It loves to find fault. Being nasty gives it life.

This Gremlin wants you to believe that as soon as you begin writing, you must show sparks of brilliance, if not entire conflagrations.

And so, when you read back over your first scribblings and find that they're actually pretty scrappy, pedestrian and maybe don't make much sense?

"Well," says the **Hyper-Critical Gremlin**, "that just proves that you're no good. You're only humiliating yourself."

Even experienced writers have to endure this vindictive creature watching their every move, one eye always on their technique.

"Didn't you say you were a writer?" it'll ask, sniffily. "Wow, you're really bad! Don't let anyone see that mess or they'll find out that you've been winging it and that actually, *you suck at this*!"

What a complete drainer. With this drip-drip-dripping negativity, belittling your every effort, you'll be so busy dodging poisoned barbs it'll be hard to focus on the road ahead.

Most of us do not enjoy criticism of our most vulnerable selves; it hurts too much. Is it any surprise that many writers can't take this constant barrage of abuse? That many creative travellers wearily conclude that the Gremlin is right; that they *do* suck at this and they should stop? And as these writers execute a U-turn and head for home, the Gremlin tucks its hands behind its head, relaxes and smiles. Job done.

The **Hyper-Critical Gremlin** works in partnership with the **Imposter Syndrome Gremlin**, and yes, sure enough, there's old **Imposter**, standing at your front door, a self-satisfied smile on its face, as it bellows, "Welcome back. See! I *told* you you weren't a writer!"

BEGINNER'S SHAME

You'll know if you've encountered the **Hyper-Critical Gremlin** because you'll remember being absolutely disgusted with your writing efforts.

You may find yourself enjoying the act of writing but when it comes to reading back over your work, you're appalled by your lumpy prose, your terrible grammar and how utterly you've failed to translate the wondrous vision in your mind into words on paper.

And because feeling really terrible at something is not an enjoyable experience, you may quickly conclude that the Gremlin is right: you're no good at this and being no good at something means you should give up. Right?

If all you are going to write is utter rubbish, why bother?

IT'S ALL BEEN SAID

Another way you'll know the **Hyper-Critical Gremlin** is present is if you find yourself thinking, "I have nothing original to write, there are no new ideas, everything has already been said." But that's not *you* thinking that thought; it's a classic Gremlin at work. The **Hyper-Critical Gremlin** uses this approach to deflate your enthusiasm by telling you that things are pointless, you should stop before you start, you haven't got what it takes to be original, and so, yet again, why bother?

WHAT IF
You may also find yourself 'what-iffing':

> What if… people think I'm useless?
> What if… I'm not talented enough?
> What if… nothing comes of all my effort?

'What if' thinking generates the anxiety and fear that gives you permission to let yourself off the hook, to not try.

And so, you quit.

WHY THE HYPER-CRITICAL GREMLIN IS SO PERSUASIVE
The **Hyper-Critical Gremlin** has different techniques depending on how much experience you have of the writing process.

If you are a beginner, then all this Gremlin has to do to make you quit is cause you to forget one simple fact:

You're a beginner. Which means, you're supposed to be shit at this.

The beginnings of anything – whether that's your first creative project or the early drafts of your 10th novel – are supposed to be a mess.

Say, you wanted to learn the violin. You pick up the instrument with your favourite concerto running through your head and you attempt to replicate it. All that comes out is a chorus of caterwauling. But that's okay, isn't it? After all, how are you supposed to know how to play the violin? You've only just started!

Yet, with writing, we expect so much more from ourselves. And when our first attempts are the written equivalent of cat-yowls, we decide that *we* are the problem.

> *"I am irritated by my own writing. I am like a violinist whose ear is true, but whose fingers refuse to reproduce precisely the sound he hears within."*
> Gustave Flaubert

OUR RELATIONSHIP WITH WRITING

Many of us have grown up intimately connected to the written word. You may have written essays or reports, read books since you were children, or even have studied literature and analysed classic texts. It's an art form that we feel we know. Because of this, we mistakenly assume that creative writing should come easily to us, when in fact this kind of writing is an entirely new skill set. Sure, you can transfer some of what you've learned in the past (just as a violin player might pick up their lessons more quickly if they already know another instrument) but still, it's different. Different enough that, when you first start out, you must treat yourself as an absolute beginner. And what's the hallmark of an absolute beginner? That they're pretty bad at the thing they're trying to do.

This is one of the main secrets of being a writer: you have to develop a high tolerance for bad work because this isn't just a state that beginners experience. All writers have to write bad work before they can begin to write good work.

ICING THE CAKE BEFORE IT'S BAKED

We hate being bad at something. Whether you're an absolute beginner or an established author, we'd all quite like to get to the bit where our writing is shiny and amazing, and we can be proud of it. That's just human nature.

But to expect this stage to come at the beginning is a bit like expecting to ice the cake, decorate it with sprinkles and adorn it with a multi-coloured unicorn, all before you've even got the flour out of the cupboard.

Creativity doesn't emerge from us fully formed and pretty. It starts as a mess and we work from there, taking it through the various stages until it becomes as close to our idealised version as we are currently capable of. But – and we will say this again because it is so, so important – to get through these stages requires us to develop a tolerance for mess.

The more times you go through this process, the more you will trust that this apparent mess has the capacity to turn into something amazing. But what if you're new to it, or it's been a while since you've done it? Well, chances are you'll look at your blob, then look at the picture of the sparkly unicorn cake that is your end-goal, and conclude that you suck.

This is a simple misunderstanding of how creativity works. When we look at other people's creative efforts, we only see the end result – the tip of a very, very large iceberg. We do not see the work, the graft, the false starts, the huge blob of cake mix. That favourite novel of yours, do you think it always looked like that? That it always flowed so effortlessly? Hell no. It was once a pile of random notes, a terrible first draft, perhaps even a completely different story.

The author turned up at the page, month after month, and shaped their raw materials until, via persistence and commitment, they turned that mess into something beautiful.

GETTING PAST THE HYPER-CRITICAL GREMLIN

As is often the case, the **Hyper-Critical Gremlin** might act tough but really, it's just terrified of failure.

And since the best way never to fail is never to create anything, well, this creature is going to make damn sure that you do not continue on your creative journey. Which is why it'll nag at you until you swerve the car over to the side of the road and hand it the keys.

Now, to be straight; the **Hyper-Critical Gremlin** might always be with you. Being creative almost always involves fear and vulnerability. It's just part of the deal. So, we're not trying to destroy this Gremlin. What we need is to soothe it enough so that you can carry on with your journey.

AGREEING WITH THE GREMLIN

You know how some martial arts experts teach students how to use an opponent's strength against them? Well, that's what we suggest you do with the **Hyper-Critical Gremlin**.

The next time you start to write, and your Gremlin tells you that you're terrible, simply say, "Yes! You're right! That's because I'm *supposed* to be!"

Surprised? Maybe you thought you should be telling your Gremlin it is wrong, that actually your stuff is amazing, thank you very much! But there's no power in that, because right now, it's probably not true and you won't believe it. Your work probably isn't any good. Not yet, anyway. And that's perfectly okay because it means you are exactly where you are meant to be in this process.

There's far more power in challenging the Gremlin's erroneous suggestion that you should be brilliant right from the start, which is just a ruse to make you feel depressed and disheartened and give up.

So, from now on, every time your Gremlin tells you that your writing stinks, you just smile sweetly and say, "Of course! Don't you know? You can't ice a cake before it's baked."

SHITTY FIRST DRAFTS

We are great believers in something the wonderful writer Anne Lamott calls 'Shitty First Drafts'[vi]. Some people also call them 'the vomit draft'. You may gather by the language that we are not talking about something beautiful here.

Writing a shitty first draft involves redefining the work you're doing. Instead of telling yourself that you are writing a wonderful story, remind yourself of your real mission: to get to the end of a shitty first draft.

You can give yourself some helpful guidelines to achieve this. Such as, it doesn't have to be good, it doesn't even have to make much sense. It just has to be done.

Then, every time you catch yourself fretting about word use or lamenting your clunky plot, remind yourself that *it doesn't matter*. You cannot edit a blank page.

Your first draft is all about getting the raw material down so that you can start to shape it. Any little whispers from your Gremlin telling you that you're doing it all wrong are just attempts to make you stop, so that you won't get to the end of a first draft – because the end of a first draft is *very* powerful.

UNIQUELY YOU

And what about the suggestion that there is nothing new to be written? That all the good ideas are gone? Well, yes and no! Researchers have concluded that only six core story trajectories exist onto which more complex narratives are built. So in many ways we're all telling the same stories, over and over.

But what our Gremlin fails to grasp is that it is in the *building* of these narratives that each writer brings their own unique voice.

A voice that is made up of all the experiences, beliefs, values and relationships which that person and *only* that person has.

We all filter the world through our own unique kaleidoscope, so if 100 people wrote a story about a table in a museum, you'd get 100 different stories.

Infinite possibility. Inexhaustible points of view. Meaning that the world is waiting for your story to be written because it hasn't heard it yet; not the way you're going to tell it.

PROMISE YOUR GREMLIN A JOB

The interesting thing about your **Hyper-Critical Gremlin** is that – once you've finished a draft of your creative project and want to start redrafting your work, ready to send to competitions, agents and publishers – you might actually benefit from its keen eye and brutal opinions.

While this overly-keen, nit-picking creature is a total killjoy when it comes to early drafts, it can be of great use when you're editing later versions.

That's because the editing and redrafting stage requires you to look dispassionately at your work – to axe scenes, to change characters and to kill your darlings (which means losing chunks of prose, beloved characters or even entire plotlines to which you are deeply attached but don't work for the story) – and when it comes to killing darlings, who is a better hired gun than this dude?

So, when it pipes up in the early stages of your journey, just tell **Hyper-Critical** that you *do* need its help, but just not right now. Tell it to take a nap and you'll wake it up when you're ready.

By the end of this chapter, you've learned that it's okay for your initial writing efforts to be terrible, because they are supposed to be that way. All you need to do is carry on, developing a tolerance for the mess that is creativity along the way, and trusting that your early-stage writing is cake mix. That it is in the process of turning into something wonderful.

And because you've finally got the **Hyper-Critical Gremlin** off your back, you're starting to really get into the journey now. You're loving the process and actually feel like a writer!

But are you the *right* kind of writer? Uh-oh.

Say hello to our next glamour-puss of a Gremlin.

CHAPTER THREE QUICK MAP

- You may sabotage yourself by insisting that your work should be great right from the start

- You're in the early stages – of course your writing isn't good!

- Being a writer involves developing a tolerance for 'mess'

- Quieten your Gremlin by agreeing with it – yes, you're supposed to be shit at this. That's because you're just starting out or only on your first draft!

- If the Gremlin suggests there's nothing original left to write, tell it that all writers bring their unique experiences to the page

- While a hindrance in early drafts, your Hyper-Critical Gremlin's laser-sharp focus will come in handy at the editing and polishing stages

HOW AUTHORS BECOME UNSTOPPABLE #3
Sarah Tierney, author of Making Space (Sandstone Press)

When I read through the first draft of Making Space, after taking a couple of months off from it, I was overwhelmed by how much of it didn't work, or wasn't quite right. I thought it would be best to scrap the whole book and start again with something new.

The idea of starting afresh was very tempting. Before you begin writing a book, you can imagine that you're going to create something amazing. The reality – that it's nowhere near amazing – can be very disheartening.

The thing that stopped me starting something completely new was knowing that I'd probably feel just as disappointed when I read it through – and I'd be no closer to writing a good book. I didn't want to spend my life writing first drafts without moving forwards.

I managed to stay motivated by listing the things I didn't like about the first draft, working out why I didn't like them, and most importantly, how I could change them. Once I'd pinpointed where the problems were, it didn't feel like the whole book was wrong – just certain elements of it.

Nowadays I see this 'I hate my book' phase as just part of the process of making it as good as I can. Once I've moved from hating it to fixing it, I start to feel a lot better.

CHAPTER FOUR

The Too-Cool-For-School Gremlin who says:

"Your work isn't proper writing."

TRUSTING YOUR CREATIVE JOURNEY

So far on this journey, you've challenged the notion that you're not a writer, realised that you don't need to feel fully prepared before you start, and quietened down the nagging voice that insists that if your early efforts aren't brilliant, you should just give up.

This usually leads to a pleasant period where you get into the rhythm of your writing, find you are enjoying yourself, and maybe even get a little taste of that 'flow state' artists are always banging on about.

And then, as though it can sense your burgeoning happiness, who should appear on the road, thumb out, hitching a ride? It's the **Too-Cool-For-School Gremlin**.

You stop for this Gremlin because it appears so impressive, well-travelled, knowledgeable, super-sophisticated. It looks like it'll be a fun and useful travelling companion on your creative road trip, with its literary style and fabulous, arty clothes.

But once **Too-Cool** has got itself settled in to your passenger seat, that's when it'll start name dropping. It'll mention magazines and journals and publishing deals. Broadsheet culture sections and highbrow fiction prizes.

It'll point out all the other, more exciting journeys it has hitched a ride on. Then this Gremlin will peer down the end of its nose at the road ahead of you, and say disdainfully, "Honey, are you sure this is the way you want to go?"

Too-Cool-For-School Gremlin is a snobby, judgemental creature whose only aim in life is to divert you away from your own path and onto someone else's.

> "Writing chick-lit? Oh, darling that's beneath you."
> "Poetry that *rhymes*? That's not going to win the Pulitzer is it?"
> "A crime series? Don't you want to be taken seriously?"
> "Fantasy? Oh, dear me; no, no, no."

And so on.

You may try to pay no attention, but as you steadfastly continue on your journey, the **Too-Cool-For-School Gremlin** is in your ear, pointing out the routes of other, lauded, critically-acclaimed, successful writers, and telling you that, "If you want to be a real writer, well, honestly, it looks very much like you're on the wrong road entirely."

Sometimes this Gremlin will hitch a ride with someone else, whose writing we deem to be 'worthy' – an exciting new poet maybe or an experimental fiction writer. Is our Gremlin silent then?

Oh no. In this case, it'll just switch up its game, telling the poor beleaguered soul that it's all very well pursuing those noble creative goals, but what the hell is the point if it's never going to make them any money?

You see, with a **Creative Gremlin** you really can't win.

SOMEONE ELSE'S DREAM

You'll know you've fallen foul of the **Too-Cool-For-School Gremlin** if you have taken a turn in your creative road trip and begun to write a story that you think is 'proper writing'. Writing that other people will approve of, that you believe has 'worth' or is the kind of writing that you think the market wants, but which doesn't make your heart sing.

The further you push on with this supposedly worthy journey, the less enthusiastic you'll get and the more sluggish the journey will become. But hey, you're writing something that will impress others, so it's all good, right? Except, no, it's not good.

Because, if you've listened to the **Too-Cool-For-School Gremlin** and taken one of these suggested 'superior' routes that all those other people seem to love and admire so much, you might splutter along for a while but all you're really doing is travelling further and further away from the source of your own unique creativity.

The journey will become increasingly arduous. In the end, you'll begin to wonder why creating feels so much like dull work rather than play. You wonder whether it's even worth doing at all.

You might even give up.

> *"Don't bend; don't water it down; don't try to make it logical; don't edit your own soul according to the fashion. Rather, follow your most intense obsessions mercilessly."*
> Franz Kafka

WHY THE TOO-COOL-FOR-SCHOOL GREMLIN IS SO PERSUASIVE

Many of us have grown accustomed to always trying to present an idealised version of our self in order to please or impress everyone else.

And let's face it, it's not getting any easier. Thanks to our immersion in technology, we're living in a world in which *appearing* to be happy and successful can often seem like a bigger priority than actually *being* happy and successful.

We have social media sites continually refreshing stories of magazine-worthy accomplishments and all we see is the polished image – we don't see the emotions and situations behind the staged shot. So, we try to make our own life into something that looks equally impressive. And hey, who cares if it makes us miserable? So long as everyone else thinks we're amazing!

DIFFERENT STROKES

What does this have to do with thinking our writing is not 'proper' writing?

Seeking approval from the world (known as having an 'external locus of approval') causes us to value what other people think of us over what what we actually enjoy.

It puts the provider of good feelings somewhere outside of us. Ultimately, this means we often end up trading-in the much deeper, more enduring pleasure of being authentic and experiencing a state of flow for the short-lived, empty pleasure of social 'strokes'.

WHAT ARE SOCIAL STROKES?

Eric Berne's theory of transactional analysis defines a 'stroke' as a 'fundamental unit of social action'[vii]. Berne believed that we seek strokes as recognition that we're acknowledged, that we have significance. We need strokes to feel that we're alive. A stroke occurs when one person verbally or non-verbally recognises another person, either positively or negatively e.g. a smile, a frown, a compliment or insult.

For the purposes of our point, we are talking here about positive strokes, and how our natural tendency to try to get them might lead us off our creative path.

Writing can be a lonely pursuit. Often, we have to push on without much validation. So the desire to seek out the approval and recognition of others to make it all feel worthwhile is completely understandable.

But that sometimes means we pretend to be something we are not, to like things we don't, or not to enjoy the things we love.

WE NEED TO TALK ABOUT GUILTY PLEASURES

We really don't enjoy the term 'guilty pleasures'. All it does is perpetuate the notion of 'socially sanctioned' enjoyment. That there are cool, intellectual or impressive things that others will approve of, and other stuff that we either have to pretend we don't enjoy or re-package into a naughty indulgence so that we can admit in company to liking it.

We can all fall foul of this because, as humans, we have a predisposition to presenting our 'best' selves to others, to increase our chances of belonging and staying in the tribe. So, we've been there. We've rearranged the books on our shelves to show a more intellectual, less self-help-addicted side of ourselves.

Pretended, when asked, that our favourite film is the oddball classic *Harold and Maude* when really, it's *The Muppets Christmas Carol*. Tuned the radio to a classical music station when we're really dying to get some 90s pop music blasting.

And it's fine. It's normal to want to show yourself in what you imagine to be your best light.

But you know what? When it comes to creativity, your best light is your true light. And creativity knows that.

Which is why your creativity does not give one single fuck about what other people think. The opinions of others – whoever the hell these 'others' even are – mean absolutely nothing to your creative flow. Zero. It's distraction, noise, bullshit, just getting in the way of the art that you are destined to make.

The only thing that your creativity cares about is your genuine enthusiasm.

PASSION IS POWER

Your enthusiasm is the fuel for your creative journey and if there's one thing you're going to need to finish this trip, it's fuel.

Because yes, writing is joyful, but writing is also graft. Especially if you are embarking on a big project such as a novel. And it's your authentic passion, your odd little preoccupations, your heartfelt love of the themes and the subject matter of the thing that you're writing about that will afford you the power and momentum to see your project through to the end.

You cannot use someone else's passions to power your journey. It just doesn't work that way.

SELF-APPROVED

As a writer who has pledged to journey along their creative path, it's your job to notice when you have sought recognition from elsewhere and whether it's at odds with the route your creativity wants to take. And then it's up to you to decide if it is worth the sacrifice. Would you rather have these fleeting strokes of approval than the long-term satisfaction of creating a piece of art that is unique and true to you?

We believe that it's important to master the skill of looking inside yourself rather than outside to judge whether what you're doing is authentic.

Not only does this mean that you will stay on your own track – even when faced with news of another prize-winning novelist or when someone looks down their nose at your genre of choice – it also means that you will build your inner strength and self-reliance.

Creativity wants us to be strong in ourselves. Really, it *needs* us to be. When you write, it's not like having a job. You won't get an appraisal that tells you how well you've done. You won't get a bonus. You don't get the same kind of affirmation you get in the everyday world.

Eventually, if you persist, then you will start to get recognition for your efforts. But you can't depend on this as a reason for writing. You have to be your own champion.

As we've mentioned, nobody cares that you write this story anywhere near as much as you do. And, if you're depending on external motivation to carry on…well, after the initial encouragements of your friends and family, you might eventually find yourself running dry.

But if the motivation to pursue your project comes entirely from your own enthusiasm and determination; if it comes from the feeling that only you can create this thing and if you don't create it, it will never exist…? Then you won't need the approval or validation of anyone else to drive you forwards. You'll have all the motivation that you need inside yourself.

Which means nothing can stop you.

GETTING PAST THE TOO-COOL-FOR-SCHOOL GREMLIN

As usual, though it may not intend to be, the **Too-Cool-For-School Gremlin** is actually pretty helpful. It helps to reveal all of the many preconceptions that we carry inside us about what we should be and do.

Whenever our minds present us with a 'should', say – for instance: "I should be writing literary short stories" (when really your heart lies in detective fiction) – it can be helpful to stop and think: says who?

Like the beliefs that we started to form when we were too young to make sense of the world and our place in it, *shoulds* are little chunks of code; messages we've been given that we tend to internalise and regard as fact.

But if we dig deeper, we might find that those beliefs about the kind of thing we should be writing aren't ours at all. They're someone else's. And just like that false information we internalised about not being a writer, so this information is also inaccurate. And if it doesn't apply to us, then it is time to let it go.

But if those *shoulds* aren't relevant to us anymore, how do we know what is?

WHAT DO YOU LOVE?

We believe that love and creativity are almost indistinguishable. Which means, if you pursue the things you love, your creativity will follow.

Take a moment to think about your top ten favourite novels and ten favourite films. Maybe jot them down.

These are the ones that you would curl up with at home if you were feeling in need of a jolt of inspiration or a happy-boost. That you watch or read over and over again. That stay in your memory long after you finished them. Or those with a plot that you find yourself still detailing to people whose eyes glazed over a good ten minutes ago.

Notice if, even as you think about them, you find yourself trying to 'improve' your list with titles that sound more impressive, cool, clever or arty.

Notice how strong the urge to filter yourself is even when no one is watching! Decide that, since this is solely about getting to know your creativity, 'improving' your list is utterly pointless. All you're doing is interrogating your tastes to find the things that perfectly sum up *you*.

Once you have your list in mind, consider what these works have in common. Take a while to really explore this. Be curious about any links that you can find.

Maybe several of your favourites have a female protagonist, or a melancholy feel? Maybe they share a sense of subtlety, humour or a particular location? Are they all set in the future? Do many of them have deep emotional themes or are they explosions of screwball silliness? Romance or tragedy? The clues you discover here will help you tune into what excites and interests you most.

This is such valuable information. Once you start to pay attention to what you actually like, you can follow this trail of breadcrumbs and they will lead you to your natural creative home.

FIND YOUR TRIBE

One way to begin the switch from an external locus of approval to an internal one is to find other people who love the same things you do. In this way, you can receive validation or strokes whilst doing work that also serves your true creation vision. This might mean, for instance, finding a group of Sci-Fi writers online rather than posting your ideas on Twitter where anyone can judge them.

Or going on a course for writers of your chosen genre rather than showing your work to a group of old university friends who do not share your taste in fiction. But be aware that, even amongst people who celebrate your line of work, the ultimate validation of whether what you are doing is worth it is always going to lie with you. This is the muscle to build. This is your creative freedom.

YOU DO YOU

Do you want to have an edge as a writer? Then investigate and learn to respect what you love. Because, whilst paying attention to awards and trends might help you to write a book that many others could write, if you focus instead on the things that you love most, then you'll create something utterly unique that could only ever have come from you.

And next time **Too-Cool-For-School Gremlin** tells you that it thinks you've chosen the wrong route, you can tell it to sit back and relax. True artists don't follow paths that have been trodden before. You're doing this *your* way, which means you're taking a journey unlike any seen before. And that makes this experience a very special one indeed.

By the end of this chapter, you've delved into the subjects, genres and themes that make your creativity come alive and now you're beginning to trust your creative journey. In fact, you should be cruising along and making excellent progress. Woohoo!

But hold on…is that a hot dog stand? You are pretty hungry, maybe you should stop off and buy one. And hey, isn't it about time you pumped up the tyres? No? Well, didn't someone mention there was a car show taking place just over that hill? What was that? Did someone say ice cream?

Just when you were starting to make progress, it seems like there are a million little distractions.

Strap yourself in. You're about to meet your next Gremlin.

CHAPTER FOUR QUICK MAP

- You might tell yourself that your writing isn't 'proper' or 'worthy'

- This is putting the 'locus of approval' outside of yourself and instead onto the people you assume are judging you

- Creativity doesn't care about what's worthy or cool, it only cares about passion and enthusiasm

- Get to know yourself and pay attention to what you love – it's what forms your unique creativity and makes you special

- Quieten your Too-Cool-For-School Gremlin by reminding it that real artists don't follow other people's supposedly 'accepted' paths

HOW AUTHORS BECOME UNSTOPPABLE #4
Caroline Hulse, author of The Adults (Orion)

I've given up writing thousands of times. I still nearly give up regularly. Writing may be my full-time job now, but some days the words just don't flow.

For me, a book is a series of false starts and reversals. I have to remind myself that, if I write through the words that don't work, if make myself just sit there and do it, eventually I'll reach a conclusion. Either I'll find what I'm writing isn't working and needs to be set aside (painful) or I'll find I've started getting excited again (much more fun).

It's not just the internal pressures that can demoralise. Every time I finished a book and got the round of consistent rejection from agents, I gave up. I threw myself into my day job until another idea came to me that I just couldn't ignore, and the whole cycle restarted.

It took twenty years and five books to get a publishing deal, probably partly because I got better along the way, and partly I took the advice 'write what you want to read' literally. My writing didn't fit a particular genre, so it was a leap of faith for a busy, commercial agent to take me on. And there are definitely paths to a much easier life out there. But eventually an agent took a risk on me and, now, people like my writing for being 'different'. Funny old world.

I'm reluctant to give advice, it's so subjective. And luck and timing play a big part. But if you're going to become a professional author, you will experience false starts, rejection and confidence battles on a daily basis. And, for me, that's all part of the process. Without those setbacks, I could never create something I am proud of.

CHAPTER FIVE

The Procrastination Gremlin who says:

"Hey, wouldn't it be more fun to do…literally anything else?!"

STICKING WITH YOUR CREATIVE JOURNEY

You're now more than halfway through your creative journey. You've got past some pretty heavyweight Gremlins and you're able to immerse yourself in your creativity, knowing how to quieten those nagging voices.

But then other certain intrusive thoughts begin to appear. Like, you feel compelled to watch the first auditions of every candidate on 'American Idol'. Or you notice that your curtains need hoovering. Or you need to plot your daily coffee consumption on an Excel spreadsheet.

Introducing, the **Procrastination Gremlin**.

This Gremlin can sense when it looks like you might actually be en route to completing your creative journey and that's when it pops up in the middle of the road with a big sign offering half-price ice cream sundaes, if you'll just stop the car right here.

The **Procrastination Gremlin**'s only job is to stop you from creating. It wants you off the road. And it has a million and one tricks up its sleeve to achieve that.

The weird thing is, even though you may have been thoroughly enjoying your creative project up until that point, as soon as the **Procrastination Gremlin** shows up, its suggestions seem to make such sense.

> *Of course* I should be rearranging the children's sock drawers.
> *Of course* I have to reply to that email from Great Uncle Herbert.
> *Of course* it is imperative that I waste two hours immersed in a Twitter spat between two people I've never met.

The distraction may be fun, and feel like a naughty diversion. Or it might involve drudgery, and feel like a penance. Frankly, the resourceful **Procrastination Gremlin** doesn't really care what it does to get you to quit; as long as you do. It's betting that once you stop off on your journey, you'll never start again.

Procrastination affects beginners and long-term writers alike. The **Procrastination Gremlin** doesn't care how many journeys you've completed. It knows that no writer, beginner or veteran, ever truly escapes the lure of procrastination. All our Gremlin needs to do is find the perfect placard to entice us with…

THE THIEF OF TIME
You'll know if you've been accosted by the **Procrastination Gremlin** because, although you definitely sat down intending to do some writing, you find yourself deep-cleaning your oven.

If every time you get back on your creative road trip, **Procrastination Gremlin** pops up with yet another enticing sign and you dutifully pull over, well, chances are one of two things will happen.

One is that you'll lose your connection to your creativity, your writing will start to stall and you'll convince yourself that this writing malarkey was a terrible idea. That you're not meant to be on this creative journey anyway. And you'll turn the car around and go back home.

The other is that you'll stay on the same journey forever, writing the same stories for years, making only miniscule progress before the **Procrastination Gremlin** appears and drags you off on yet another flight of fancy.

And, in fact, the second outcome is worse, because you'll really believe you are still on your way to finishing a piece of writing, little realising that **Procrastination** can keep you occupied forever.

> *"We are so scared of being judged that we look for every excuse to procrastinate."*
> Erica Jong, Seducing the Demon[viii]

WHY THE PROCRASTINATION GREMLIN IS SO PERSUASIVE

We know that procrastination is a problem. But why? I mean, if we have already decided that writing is something we want to do, why are we so easily distracted by other activities that don't bring us anywhere near as much satisfaction and joy?

Well, it turns out that this fickle behaviour can be down to Low Frustration Tolerance, or LFT for short.

LFT is a term which was coined by psychologist Albert Ellis, one of the early forefathers of Cognitive Behavioural Therapy[ix]. It describes how our inability to tolerate discomfort causes us to avoid that which we can't resolve quickly and easily.

What does that mean for writers trying to complete a creative project?

It means that if we're not aware of LFT being at play, then whenever we're faced with the uncertainty of the blank page, the challenge of beginning, or the difficulty of resolving an issue or problem in our work, we'll procrastinate. We'll avoid the discomfort. We'll find something that will deliver instant gratification instead.

ZERO TOLERANCE GAME

This explains why, even if our writing is going well, procrastination can still be a problem. Because the thing about writing is, unless you're penning limericks (and maybe even then), it's not something that can often be 'resolved quickly and easily'. As discussed in previous chapters, creativity asks us to let go of trying to control, to ignore the **Hyper-Critical Gremlin**, to follow our passions and see where they lead, to get comfortable with mess, and to make our peace with being terrible at something.

All of that is wonderful but none of it is particularly quick or easy.

At least not in the beginning. And even once you've nailed the initial learning stages, you'll still be puzzling over plot, theme, language, ideas, characters etc for the rest of your writing life – because that's the job. Being a writer means to be out of your depth most of the time.

Which is why when we are faced with a writing session, we often go looking for something that feels more manageable instead.

Trouble is, this is a short-term fix that just leads to long-term misery. We get our little dopamine hit but there's no satisfaction because we're not able to develop projects sustainably in the way we want. And if you're going to complete your creative journey, you need to be able to endure short-term difficulty to get to the finish line.

So how do you learn to stay focused, resisting the **Procrastination Gremlin** as it pesters you along your creative journey with its enticements to stop and have some fun or take care of some supposedly urgent task?

GETTING PAST THE PROCRASTINATION GREMLIN
You're probably getting used to us telling you by now that our Gremlins aren't the wicked beasties that they might at first appear to be.

And the **Procrastination Gremlin** is no exception. It's only standing out there on that road waving its signs around because it is terrified of creativity and the threat it poses.

Let us explain.

Humans are ancient beings and we carry our ancestors' instincts: When we perceive threat our body responds with a great surge of adrenaline preparing us for fight/flight/freeze.

The key word we want to bring to your attention is *perceive*.

For our ancestors, it was pretty easy. See a woolly mammoth? Get the hell outta here!

But for us? I said I would write for an hour this morning. Get the hell outta here!

It isn't the same kind of threat at all, and yet our limbic system may be flooding our body with the same hormones that induce panic and fear.

Why?

Because we perceive a threat. We don't know how the session is going to go. We don't know if we're going to pull off what we hoped to. We don't know if we're going to mess it up and threaten our sense of identity as a competent, creative, talented writer.

So, we panic, like a Neanderthal that's just seen a woolly mammoth.

But notice again that we say *perceive* to be a threat.

This is good news.

Because perception is simply another way of saying 'a story that we're telling ourselves'. And, as we have already learned, if we want to, we can change any story that we're telling ourselves.

NOTICE

If you find that you're agitated, distracted and can't sit still, then your limbic brain is probably stimulated.

The first crucial thing to do is simply notice that this is happening, without judgement. Say to yourself, "Oh, I notice that I really want to go and sort that ironing out right now instead of writing this scene. How interesting."

The next step is to take a few deep breaths, particularly focusing on the out-breath. The out-breath activates the parasympathetic nervous system, which turns off the flight/fight/freeze hormones, settling your system down so it can think more clearly.

Next, the free writing practice we mentioned in Chapter One really comes into its own. Spend five minutes journaling, pouring out what's in your head, and start to notice what you are telling yourself about why you don't want to write today.

Alternatively, you might want to approach the journaling with a prompt, asking yourself, "What is my positive intention for this session? How do I want to feel as I sit down to write?" This takes your mind away from the challenge or difficulty of what you are *producing*, and instead invites you to consider how you want to feel during the *process*; bringing you right back to the present moment. A place where you have choice and free will. Where you have the option of, well, enjoying yourself, rather than using the writing as a form of self-torture.

It's important that you don't criticise yourself for not wanting to write. It's perfectly natural. But recognising this an important first step, and will start to give you enough distance from being *in* that state to allow you to *change* your state.

TIC/TOC

Once you recognise that this is happening and have started to calm your system, you can deploy your rational brain – the calming, evidence-based, logical, reasoning brain – to counter. With a game of TIC/TOC.

Simply identify the Task Interfering Cognition (TIC) and write it on one side of a piece of paper. Then counter this with a Task Optimising Cognition (TOC) and write that on the other side of the paper. The result might look something like this:

I'm the worst writer ever.	**People have complimented me on my work.**
It's too hard, I can't do this.	**I've got past this point before. I know I can finish a piece of work.**
This is the worst story I've ever written.	**It's not finished yet. It could turn out to be the best one ever.**

REWARD YOUR EFFORTS

We've been telling you from the start that the writing process can at times be hard. So, it's important to recognise your efforts as you go along in order to help the mind associate effort with reward.

When it comes to reward, get creative and find what works best for you.

Break it down: "Once I finish my 30 minutes, I will treat myself to a coffee."

Build it up: "At the end of every month, I will reward myself with a lunch out with a friend."

Give yourself a gift: Wrap up small presents for yourself and open one each time you reach a milestone, such as every 10,000 words, or every five writing sessions successfully completed.

Whatever you do, make a point of really owning the moment. Celebrate achievements big and small. Bring your awareness to how good it feels to get to the end of that 30-minute session, or that 1,000-word goal.

Strengthen the relationship in your mind between enduring short-term frustration and gaining the satisfaction of reward. Retrain your brain, one chocolate doughnut at a time.

INTERNET ADDICTION

A side note about internet addiction. No matter how committed you might be to your project, the distraction (and dopamine hits) offered by social media sites are a major problem for writers.

If you find yourself drifting off from your work to chat

on Facebook, don't beat yourself up. Just be completely realistic about your capabilities for resisting the internet and then take action accordingly. Here are three actions that we find helpful:

1) Turn off your router for the duration of your writing session. If you have data on your phone, leave it in another room

2) Download an app (such as Freedom) that blocks access to your chosen websites for a set time period

3) Go old school – work in a café with a pen and paper (and switch off your phone!)

PROCRASTINATE WITH PURPOSE

Now, there's nothing wrong with cleaning the oven, watching TV, or chatting online. And the last thing we want to do is demonise these activities, mainly because our Gremlins see hard boundaries and tend to run at them, screaming "WHHHYYY" in a daytime soaps-like fashion. They're just like that.

So, if we create a rule that 'all procrastination is bad' then your mind may kick in to argue the toss. Because arguing the toss is, you know, more fun than doing the hard task. Yep, it's just another form of procrastination, disguised as good sense!

Better for us then that we hold soft boundaries and allow ourselves to procrastinate with purpose. How do you do that?

Aim for something truly mindless. Clean the skirting boards. Shampoo the dog. Did you know that Bill Gates used to do the washing up? You know, billionaire Bill Gates. Busy global business man. Why did he like to do his own dishes? Because he understood that the brain thrives when we let it get bored.

> "It turns out that when you get bored, you ignite a network in your brain called the "default mode." So our body goes on autopilot while we're folding the laundry or we're walking to work, but that is when our brain gets really busy. In the default mode, we connect disparate ideas, we solve some of our most nagging problems, and we do something called "autobiographical planning."
>
> "This is when we look back at our lives, we take note of the big moments, we create a personal narrative, and then we set goals and we figure out what steps we need to take to reach them."
> Manoush Zomorodi[x]

Alternatively, aim for something truly mindful. Get stuck into a colouring book. Do a jigsaw. There are jewels in getting lost in something else. If we trust our creativity to know when it might need to go wandering, then it may come back with a gem.

This might be a realisation that helps with your current project. It may be a completely new idea, something that brings energy and enthusiasm into the field. Or it may just be that the brain was signalling to you that it needed some breathing space to delve deeper into this unconscious bank of resources. (More of this in Chapter 6.)

Finally, experiment with giving yourself permission not to write. If you hear yourself angling to procrastinate then acknowledge it and say, "I choose not to write." Really own the decision. Nothing is more disarming to a Gremlin than agreement. And in our experience, the moment you give yourself permission not to write, the very next thought you'll hear is, "Oh, but I really want to!"

> *"…how curious this process of writing is, I must have no enthusiasm, no pride in whether I can do it. There seems always to be a feeling of futility, that I have nothing to say, and usually I try to get away from this by force, by looking for something to say, and then my head begins to ache;*
>
> *but if I accept this futility, give up my purpose to write, and yet don't run away into some other activity, just sit still and feel myself to be no good – then the crystallisation begins – after the corruption, blackness, despair."*
> Marion Milner, An Experiment in Leisure[xi]

So maybe, armed with this new information, the next time the **Procrastination Gremlin** waves a sign in front of you, instead of screeching to a halt and abandoning your vehicle, you'll just calmly check the time and say, "I'm fine for distractions right now thanks. But I'll meet you in 40 minutes for an ice cream sundae."

Okay, so by now on your journey, you are well prepared for the next time the **Procrastination Gremlin** pops up in your path.

You know that you have the tools to counter those urges to stop writing, and because you understand why this is happening, you're able to spend longer and longer immersed in your creative work.

Which is wonderful, right? Right. Except, if you find that you've gone from one extreme to the other – that from hardly writing at all you're now doing very little else – then, alas, there's a good chance you may have been hijacked by our next Gremlin.

CHAPTER FIVE QUICK MAP

- You may find yourself procrastinating instead of writing

- This can be due to Low Frustration Tolerance

- You may perceive the challenges writing brings as a threat

- You can use TIC/TOC to reframe how you think about writing

- You can use rewards to motivate yourself

- If you are going to procrastinate, then do it mindlessly, mindfully or with permission

HOW AUTHORS BECOME UNSTOPPABLE #5
Pippa James, author of The Happiness Project (Bookouture)

I get stuck all the time. Usually it happens less when I'm in the middle of a book and more excited about it, but there are still times when I'm on the sofa in my lounge, feeling a bit tired and lacking the energy to get up and write. There are several ways I get around it:

1) Bribery - I have a really nice box of Hotel Chocolat chocs on my desk, but I have to 'earn' one of them with a decent amount of work.

2) Help from others – mostly my husband giving me a look as he switches the TV to something I don't like (I can't argue, because I should be writing!).

3) Tricking myself – on my way home from work or while I'm waiting to pick my kids up from parties etc, I sit in a pub with my laptop or I arrange to meet a writer friend in a pub. There's nothing else to do, I have to write, I always make some progress even if I've had to stare at the screen for half an hour first!

4) I try to remember that I enjoy it. Not every second, but it's always worth it!

CHAPTER SIX

The Tyrant Gremlin who says:

"If you're going to do it, it has to hurt."

ENJOYING YOUR CREATIVE JOURNEY

So, you're writing and it's going well. You're getting hundreds of words down and plenty of hours in. You've really committed to your creative journey. You're loving this amazing feeling and you never want it to end.

This is a wonderful time. But it's also a tricky one.

Because this is the point at which we are most vulnerable to the **Tyrant Gremlin**.

The **Tyrant Gremlin** opens our car door and orders us to budge over to the passenger seat. Then it takes the wheel and assures us: "Don't worry, I'll make sure you get to the end of this project!"

What it doesn't add is what it's really thinking: "Even if it kills you."

And so, on you go. Soon, it'll feel like you haven't got out of the car for days. You're parched, more than a little hungry, and your eyes are burning from staring at the road ahead for so long without a break. And, by the way, when was the last time you slept?

The **Tyrant Gremlin** particularly preys on ambitious and dedicated writers. It knows that there's little chance of persuading you to give up – it can see that steely look of determination in your eyes – so this Gremlin takes another tack. It's going to manipulate that commitment, making it so that your creative road trip is one long, arduous, painful slog from which there is no respite.

Sound fun? No, thought not. But if **Tyrant Gremlin** gets its way, it'll have you believing that the only way you can complete your creative journey is if you do it this way – no breaks, no fun, just suffering.

"This is how things get done," the **Tyrant** will insist when you suggest that perhaps you could stop off for a hot chocolate or a quick nap. "There will be no stopping! No pain, no gain!"

And because you have perhaps been led to believe that nothing good can come unless it really hurts, it's easy to let **Tyrant** stay at the wheel and trust its bloody-mindedness to get you to the end of the project. No matter if you are a drained, dried out husk of a person by the time you get there…

CRACKING THE WHIP
You'll know if you have encountered the **Tyrant Gremlin** because, although you'll be making headway on your project, you'll be feeling depleted, simultaneously exhausted and manic, and more than a little joyless.

And sure, this might seem like progress. With the **Tyrant Gremlin** at the helm you may, indeed, finish your project. But it will very likely be lacking in the lightness and the joy that made you fall in love with your story in the first place.

And if you continue to create under the rule of **Tyrant**, the happiness that creativity wants to infuse you with might well be lost in the process. You may reach the finish line, but broken and wondering whether, if this is what writing requires, is it actually worth it?

WHY THE TYRANT GREMLIN IS SO PERSUASIVE

Why, you might ask, are we so keen to suffer? Why would we want to make the journey in this punishing and painful way if we could do it in a light, breezy, and laid-back fashion?

Well, for one thing, you may have noticed that we humans hate ambiguity and love certainty. We like things to be absolute, black and white. You can witness this in the realms of diet, caffeine or alcohol. Very often, we're either on the wagon or we are off it. We're either indulging ourselves to our heart's content, or we have sworn off and are feeling very pious and self-satisfied.

We love to know where we are. Who we are. Things feel easier that way.

What does this mean for our creative projects?

If we appear to be making progress with our writing, then we may start to get scared. What if we can't keep it up? What if this is just a phase? How can we make damn sure that this burst of enthusiasm or success with writing lasts? How can we be like this all the time?

That's when we try to control it.

But the thing about true creativity is it can't be controlled. In fact, we believe that true creativity is sort of the opposite of control. It won't respond to our desperation, to our rigidity, to our neediness. Creativity doesn't exist to serve us, it wants to *play* with us.

And while creativity loves nothing more than your heartfelt commitment to nurturing your art, as soon as you start to make harsh demands of it, asking it to meet impossible deadlines, suffer ridiculous schedules or put up with inhuman working conditions: well, that's when things get tricky.

Of course, you can write stories and books with the **Tyrant Gremlin** at the wheel. You absolutely can. But, from experience, we'd argue that it's not possible to achieve the most rewarding, flow state of creativity when manic **Tyrant** is in control because the two states are the antithesis of one another.

Creativity responds to the moment and allows the journey to unfold in its own time. **Tyrant** has the route mapped out and is going to make damn sure you get there on *its* terms.

BUT YOU JUST TOLD ME TO MAKE A SCHEDULE!
Yes, we did. And we still think you should. And here's where we come to the tricky part of creativity. It isn't black and white. It's not a case of write or don't write. It's not about a binary choice between

scheduling or not scheduling. You need to find a place between those two states that works for you and for your creative flow.

Yes, you should commit to your creativity. No, you should not neglect your happiness, your joy or your health for your writing.

Creativity doesn't exist in a separate box from life. Creativity *is* life. The approaches we are applying to our creativity are the same rules that we can apply to have a happier, healthier life.

And just as in life, creativity requires us to have balance.

Of course, the **Tyrant Gremlin** isn't interested in balance. Balance is waaayyyyy too slow for this dude. All it's interested in is results.

Fast, definite results. And it doesn't care how it gets them.

But when it comes to making art, it's not just the end result that matters. We believe that a piece of creative work is made up of everything you put into it along the way. Which means that your state of being is as crucial to the finished product as each word you put down upon the page. And the healthier, more 'in flow' you can be while you are on your creative path, the more wonderful and magical the creative piece of work will be at the end. That's just how it is.

Let's go back to that cake mix. Are you going to add desperation, sleeplessness, mania and a grim sense of control to the ingredients? Or, will you opt for ease, joyfulness, and slow and steady progress? After all, these choices will determine what the cake tastes like when it's finally made.

We've said that creativity wants to play with you, so it might help to think of your creativity as a friend. Imagine you've planned to do an activity together. Then imagine you've called, hassled, and harangued that friend about the date; bullied them into the time and place that suits you (regardless of their wishes); overridden their suggestions and forced them to commit to the activity despite their attempts to bail. Sure, you get to do the activity together, which was your original aim. But does it now hold any value, after what you did to make it happen? Is this real success? And is your relationship with creativity likely to last the distance, if this is how you treat it?

THE WRONG ROUTE

Another thing about **Tyrant** is that it doesn't actually care whether the journey you are on is the *right* one for you. Its sole focus is to get to the finish line – any finish line – and get that thing checked off your To Do list.

And when **Tyrant Gremlin** has your creativity in a headlock, then your creativity can't tell you where it wants to go next. **Tyrant** will override your creative instincts and determine what it thinks is the fastest, more expedient route.

The sad thing is, there's just no way a Gremlin has a better idea for your creative project than your actual creativity does! And in trying to control it, in listening to **Tyrant**, you're cutting yourself off from the greatest supply of joy, inspiration and power that you possess.

Indeed, you may find yourself relentlessly sticking with a project, even when all the joy has gone out if it, and risk turning into an 'art-martyr', slaving away on a story that long ago lost its spark, whilst your muse is waving at you from elsewhere, wishing you would come to play on the real project that would fill you with true creative joy.

YOUR GREATEST CHALLENGE: DECIDING WHEN TO LET GO

Now, we are the first to admit that this is one of the biggest challenges of a creative life. Once it seems likely that a creative goal is in sight, it is incredibly hard for many of us not to go at that thing full pelt, to the detriment of our health, time and fully-rounded life – not to mention the quality of our output.

We are (possibly) impatient. We are very likely perfectionists and control freaks. We want to finish the story as soon as possible. We want it done now. We want to have something to show for our efforts. We want to enter that competition, pitch to that agent, get that draft to our beta reader, meet the expectations of that publisher.

And as our eyes become fixed on the finish line, we begin not to care what we might have to give up to get there.

Or whether we are even on the right road.

THE PROBLEM WITH GOALS

It is wonderful to have ambitions for your writing, but setting appropriate goals can be tricky. That's because goals tend to be about quantifiable end points. The 'what' you're going to achieve.

Whereas your creativity is more interested in the how of achieving.

We need to fall in love with the doing – with the process of making and creating art – regardless of the acclaim or recognition that we hope to get at the end.

We need to do the work, but let go of the expectations and stop fixating on the results.

Tyrant, of course, is ALL about getting to the end, all about results, and doesn't care what it takes to get you there.

HOW DO I KNOW IF THE TYRANT IS DRIVING, OR IF IT'S JUST HARD BECAUSE WRITING IS HARD?

This is one of the most difficult and most nuanced things you will ever learn as a creative person. We wish it was as simple as, "always finish what you start" or, "give up when it gets hard."

But, as we've already said, writing isn't black and white.

Very often, we will hit a pain barrier with our writing and want to go and do something else. (See 'Chapter five: **The Procrastination Gremlin**'.)

But sometimes the opposite happens. We forget to listen to our creativity, and become too rigid, too determined to stick with a project no matter what.

So, how will you know which is which?

The only way to know is through experience.

We are not suggesting that you'll be able to discern this on your first creative venture, or even your fifth, or 10th. But eventually, you'll start to see patterns developing.

The more you work with your creativity, the more you will be able to discern whether the voice in your head telling you to carry on is your **Tyrant** or your creativity.

Notice a pattern. If you always see your projects through to the end, but none of them seem to fill you with excitement, then maybe **Tyrant** has been driving.

If you continually quit projects when they get hard, even though you were actually enjoying them, then that's probably the **Completion-Phobic Gremlin** (coming up in Chapter Seven).

But if this is the first time you've felt like you need to let a project go or take a break – if the joy has gone out of it, if it doesn't make you excited anymore – then your creativity might be trying to tell you that you've taken a wrong turn. In which case it is okay to take a break, breathe, go for a walk, and see if you can't tune back into what your creativity is trying to tell you.

Because writing is graft, absolutely. But it is joyful graft. Magical graft. And it rewards and feeds us as much as it asks of us.

"Pain is inevitable. Suffering is optional."
Haruki Murakami, What I Talk About When I Talk About Running[xii]

GETTING PAST THE TYRANT GREMLIN

If you've read the previous chapters, then you might have noticed that the attitude of the **Tyrant Gremlin** is basically the opposite of the voice of creativity.

It might sound unglamorous and maybe even boring, but while your **Tyrant** wants you to burn through the night and go out in a blaze of glory, your creativity is asking you to plod, plod, plod. This is because it knows something **Tyrant** doesn't: that great works of art are made not through grim, desperate and furious striving but through trusting in steady, loving, step-by-step progress. This might look like nothing much while you're doing it, but will culminate in incredible (and solid) results.

THE TORTOISE AND THE HARE

We are sure you remember this old fable from your childhood. But just in case you don't, here's a reminder:

> A Hare mocked a Tortoise for being so much slower than him. So the Tortoise challenged him to a race. Hare readily agreed, thinking the Tortoise a fool. He went racing off ahead of the Tortoise and was soon so far ahead of him that he stopped to take a little nap. However, when he finally woke up, to his horror, he saw the Tortoise crossing the finish line ahead of him.

MAKE YOUR PEACE WITH PLODDING

In claiming your creative life, patience and plodding are key.

The problem is, our egos do not care for plodding. Plodding is not glamorous. Plodding leaves us with very little to show for our efforts much of the time. Plodding is *boring*.

This brings us back to something we touched upon when the **Too-Cool-For-School Gremlin** flagged us down in Chapter Four.

Where is our locus of approval?

True creativity asks us not to seek validation and approval from outside ourselves, and as we meet the **Tyrant Gremlin**, we can start to see why.

If we are desperate for validation, that means we are also desperate to have something to show for our efforts, ASAP. And so instead of slow and steady, we rush our work because we can't stand the isolation and loneliness of creating on our own and bearing the feelings of uncertainty.

This is perfectly understandable. Creating is *hard*. Learning to trust ourselves and developing the patience to slowly make our way through our creative project is hard. But we can do it. All we need to do is remind ourselves that we just turn up, in a slow and steady fashion, and do our work. Like the tortoise, we will get there in the end. And when we do, we'll also know that it wasn't a fluke. We'll know that we have the tools and the strength to create again and again. Ironically, by plodding, we give ourselves the certainty that **Tyrant** so badly wants – but doesn't have the patience to hold on for.

It might also help to remember what our ultimate goal is here. As humans, we are driven to create, to understand more about ourselves and the world we live in through creative expression. There is no end point or product to this process – it's its own goal, a virtuous circle.

We come to know ourselves more deeply through our creative endeavours. And our creative endeavours are richer for our exploration of ourselves. We plod, because the path to awareness, understanding and authenticity are also the destination.

"A word after a word after a word is power."
Margaret Atwood

REFUELLING

Creativity loves creativity. It can't get enough of it. And if we have been pushing our creative selves hard, then the best thing we can do is take some time out to refuel. This can mean anything from reading that sweeping epic you've had your eye on, visiting an art gallery and staring at one picture for an hour, to taking a sketchpad and going walking in the woods.

As we've said, creativity is play and therefore loves inspiration, curiosity and excitement. It loves fresh, different, new.

So, fill your eyes and ears. Notice what you're interested in and capture it.

Keep a notebook in your pocket or add a memo to your phone. Let the unconscious know that, even though you're working really hard on your own project, there's always room for it to offer you a word or a phrase, an image or a texture.

If you stay open (in playful curiosity) and organised (so you don't miss the moment) this means you'll build a smorgasbord of stimulating titbits to offer back to your own project – the chance to make a new connection or set off on an exciting new train of thought. The key is not over-thinking, over-analysing, judging or critiquing.

You're just a collector of scraps, providing your creativity with an array of material to play with. This is where it comes into its own, helping you find connections that spark a something from a whole load of nothings. Helping to bring a flash of light into the plodding.

TURNING UP TO THE PAGE
Another thing that can help with plodding is wood-chopping our goals down into really tiny ones.

We know that **Tyrant** loves a grand gesture. It wants you to finish that novel *now*! If not sooner. But creativity (a tortoise at heart) is happy taking small steps.

So, redirect your **Tyrant**. Tell it that you're the one in control and actually, the mission has changed. The end goal isn't to finish this piece of work by devoting every scrap of energy you've got. It is to develop and maintain a regular work practice that will allow you to create happily and healthily for a long, long time.

One such system is just to turn up to the page for a set time every day/week/month. Notice there's no mention of how many words written, or how marvellous those words should be! You just turn up and let creativity do the rest. You fulfil your part of the bargain, and creativity will fulfil its.

(Writer Elizabeth Gilbert has lots to say about this idea. We recommend you check out her brilliant TED talks and her wonderful book on creativity, *Big Magic*[xiii].)

And the finish line? That's not something you need to worry about. The tortoise knows that if it puts one tiny foot in front of the other, it can't fail to eventually get where it is going.

Okay, so by now on your journey you realise that pushing yourself too hard can actually take you off your creative path. You understand that you need to find balance, develop patience and make your peace with plodding.

And, eventually, having understood and incorporated everything you've learned – as promised: that plodding has paid off. The finish line is almost in sight!

There's just one last Gremlin standing in your way, and if there's one thing this creature cannot stand, it's a finisher.

CHAPTER SIX QUICK MAP

- You may mistakenly believe that achieving your writing goals has to hurt

- This means pushing yourself too hard in unhealthy ways

- Determining whether you should push on or take a break requires experience

- Creative refuelling is not only useful, but absolutely necessary

- Setting small goals and developing patience and balance is key

HOW AUTHORS BECOME UNSTOPPABLE #6
Zoe Lambert, author of The War Tour (Comma Press)

For me, the key thing is telling the difference between needless self-doubt which should be ignored, or realising a project is genuinely not working and might need some major revision or shelving.

Recently, I realised a novel I was writing wasn't working, and I was filled with anxiety about this. It was when I was visiting a friend and away from my usual routine that I realised this, and that I needed to give the work some space and perhaps write something else in the meantime.

I had to look deeply into myself and think carefully whether this was just me in a moment of self-doubt or a decision I needed to act on. But to make sure I wasn't just 'doubting myself', I shared some writing from another project with a trusted mentor, and she agreed that this project had legs, and I should leave the first novel and return to it later. This was a good, though painful decision.

CHAPTER SEVEN

The Completion-Phobic Gremlin who says:

"Almost finished? Great! Let's start something new!"

FINISHING YOUR CREATIVE JOURNEY

So, you've been writing for a while now. You've got a routine established that works for you and you're making progress. The project is one that you love and you're managing to ignore the Gremlins telling you that you're no good, that you should do it differently, that it should hurt. You know that you're on your right path because you've occasionally been experiencing that wonderful, immersive feeling of flow.

GO YOU!

So why is it, when you've got past a certain point with your manuscript, you start to feel the tickling of another great idea?

You return to your 'Work in Progress' but it seems really quite dull in comparison. And the more you think about this other idea, the more you wonder whether actually this *other* thing isn't the story you should be writing.

That's because you've picked up another, final, stowaway: the **Completion-Phobic Gremlin**.

This Gremlin's only imperative is to stop you from writing 'THE END' on the last page of your draft. It cannot let you get to the end of your project.

And because it is already aware of all the other ways that the Gremlins have tried and failed to stop you from making progress, this Gremlin has a final trick up its sleeve.

Just when you are approaching the end of your creative project, it will suggest that you go back home and start again, taking a different route. It will tell you that there's a much better journey you haven't yet taken, one that is much more suited to the real you. And it convinces you to take it.

The **Completion-Phobic Gremlin** is amazingly tenacious. It can perform this persuasive trick time and time again, so that although you are constantly on the creative road, feeling like you are making progress, you'll find that you never actually make it to the finish line of any of the journeys you've started.

This Gremlin loves targeting new writers. It knows that new writers are especially vulnerable to the idea of starting a new project, and that they can go through this cycle many, many times without even realising what is happening.

You see, this Gremlin knows one very important thing about writing: that to make real progress, you have to finish.

COULD WE START AGAIN PLEASE?

You'll know you've encountered the **Completion-Phobic Gremlin** if you have a half-dozen manuscripts or stories knocking around, but you haven't finished any of them. As soon as you get to a certain stage in each project, you'll experience the sudden urge to start something fresh.

You may have been writing for years, but you just can't seem to make any progress.

If you've encountered this Gremlin, you may find yourself losing enthusiasm for your idea just at the point when it could turn into something. Or perhaps it occurs just at the juncture where your manuscript gets a bit tricky. (It's different for everyone.)

Then your attention is attracted by the shiny new thing over there and…you're off, starting a new and wonderful project which, after a certain length of time, will also start to lose its lustre.

And then, once again, you'll begin to have doubts. You'll wonder whether this other new idea you've had is really 'the one'.

And so on, and so on.

WHY THE COMPLETION-PHOBIC GREMLIN IS SO PERSUASIVE

What is it about being deep into a writing project that makes starting another one so damn appealing?

And why the hell can't this Gremlin just let you finish something?

Well, as ever, this Gremlin is simply terrified. And the list of things it is frightened of is rather long. So, let's work through them…

THE HONEYMOON PHASE
(Fear of failing to do our idea justice)

When we first begin our writing project, we have this perfect, shining ideal in our minds and we set about trying to create it. Whilst we are experiencing these initial feelings of infatuation and bliss, our story can do no wrong. This is the first flush of 'story love'.

But the further we get into our project, the more we begin to realise that actually, we *aren't* going to be able to create the perfect idea we had in our head after all. At best, our interpretation of the story is going to be a lumpy, misshapen and imperfect beast.

The bloom is off the rose. Reality hits. And it doesn't feel great.

But understand: this is a necessary shift – from 'immature story love' to 'realistic story love'.

It is a difficult thing to come to terms with, yes, but it is the same for everyone. It's part of the job. No one can create a truly *perfect* thing. We can only do our best to come close to the ideal. And the more practice we have at finishing things, the closer we will get.

But when you first start out, you might not realise that this is just the way it is for *all* writers – new and established. You might think that because your draft is falling short of your expectations, that it is somehow the wrong idea and should be scrapped. When in fact, all that is needed is an adjustment of your expectations.

PERFECTIONISM
(Fear of judgement)

You may have found a way to enjoy the creative process and get on your path. But then, once you have some material, you find that you can't stop tinkering. It's never quite done, because it's never quite good enough. And in fact, it won't ever be, because nothing you write can be completely *perfect*.

Because, what is 'perfect' when it comes to creativity? As a writer, your job is to bring something new into the world that didn't exist before.

There is no blueprint, nothing to compare it to. What's the measure of perfect? Perfect for whom?

Perfectionism is a nice little trick of the **Completion-Phobic Gremlin**.

Finishing a project brings with it the implied possibility that we might share it with others, and thus open ourselves up to external judgement. Scary.

Now, if you're determined to finish your stories and put them out into the world, then yes, you will be judged. Not in a nasty way, just in the same way that you judge every book, television series or film that you encounter, as a way of deciding whether you enjoyed it or not. It's the bargain that you make when you create something that you want other people to experience. Not everyone is going to love what you write. But learning how to handle that takes time. It can be understandably difficult to arrive at a place where you feel able to open yourself up to criticism. To develop that thick skin.

And that's why perfectionism is such a useful stalling mechanism, keeping us spinning our wheels indefinitely.

DON'T LOOK AT ME!
(Fear of exposure)

The thing about writing is, it's very private…until it isn't. There is something about finishing a writing project that carries scary implications; the possibility that someone might eventually read and critique it. It's normal to feel nervous about others seeing your efforts laid bare on the page like that.

There may also be people whose judgement we fear. And the internal logic goes that, if we don't actually produce anything, then we don't give them anything to judge us on. Simple!

And that's true. But the fact is, if we want to put our creative works into the world, then at some point we will have to take the plunge and trust that we can handle it. That it won't kill us. That in fact, it can only make us stronger as artists. And that, actually, most of the harsh judgement we anticipate is only in our heads.

LOVING THE FRESH START
(Fear of sitting with our issues)

Who doesn't love a fresh start? As humans we're attracted to the idea of a clean page. That's why we are so fond of New Year's resolutions and why September, with its new term feeling, gives us the urge to buy new stationary and embark on new projects.

The problem is, people can become addicted to fresh starts; changing relationships, homes or jobs when things begin to get a little tough.

Now, we are not saying you should not get out of a terrible relationship/home/job/writing project if it's making you unhappy.

But what we are saying is that you take *yourself* with you.

Watch out if you're telling yourself, "Oh, it'll all be different when I am working on this *other* book." Because, yeah, it might. But you are still you. Those doubts, fears and insecurities will still arise whatever project you're working on.

So, rather than avoiding these scary feelings by continually throwing your energies into new projects, you might as well begin tackling your Gremlins on this one instead.

HANG ON, HOW DO I TELL IF THIS IS THE COMPLETION-PHOBIC GREMLIN OR THE TYRANT?

Good question. It's true, the urge to shelve your creative project might be a genuine creative decision. This could be the wrong project and therefore pushing on and ignoring your creative intuition may be just handing the wheel over to the **Tyrant Gremlin**.

Or it may be everything that we have listed above; that you are scared to reach the finish line and **Completion-Phobic Gremlin** is pulling out all the stops. As we've said in the previous chapter, the only way to know is through experience.

Observe yourself as a writer for long enough and eventually you'll start to see patterns developing. The more you work with your creativity, the more you will be able to discern who the voice in your head belongs to.

If you continually quit projects when they get hard, even though you were actually enjoying them, then that isn't **Tyrant**, that's probably the **Completion-Phobic Gremlin**.

Want to know for sure? Finish anyway. Have that experience of forcing yourself to complete a project and see how you feel at the end. Overjoyed with your writing? Then you've just busted past **Completion-Phobic**.

Feeling a little flat and joyless? Well then maybe your instinct was correct, and this wasn't the right project for you. You'll remember that feeling next time and know to pay attention to it.

GETTING PAST THE COMPLETION-PHOBIC GREMLIN
How do we get past this urge to ditch our writing projects in order to start again?

This Gremlin is all to do with maturing your relationship with writing – and it is an exciting and necessary stage to get through.

It's about adjusting expectations, understanding the landscape of writing, and coming to terms with being a perfectly imperfect person.

MAKING YOUR PEACE WITH BEING IMPERFECT
To make this point, we're bringing out the big guns: a man who was a significant driver in the field of psychotherapy back in the early 20th Century. Here is what Carl Rogers says about creativity in his work, *'Toward a Theory of Creativity.'* "The mainspring of creativity appears to be [...] man's tendency to actualize himself, to become his potentialities. The tendency to express and activate

all the capacities of the organism [. . .] may become deeply buried under layer after layer of encrusted psychological defences." [xiv]

Or put another way: we're driven to create to know ourselves more deeply and yet fear routinely stops us from trying.

Sound familiar? Think of the Gremlins you've met so far; out to sabotage you by telling you you're not an artist, you're terrible at writing, you should be doing it differently, that making art should hurt.

They all seem pretty vindictive on first encounter, but as we have seen, they're really just driven by fear.

Don't try, don't risk it, don't expose yourself – people will judge, laugh, ridicule, belittle or shame you. Blimey. It's no wonder the **Completion-Phobic Gremlin** is the most tenacious of the lot.

Finishing a piece of work can feel like the scariest and biggest risk of all.

But, as Rogers says, we're *driven* to create, to express, to understand who we are and what being alive means to us through individual creative expression.

Rogers also says:

"Perhaps the most fundamental condition of creativity is that the source or locus of evaluative judgment is internal. The value of his product is, for the creative person, established not by the praise and criticism of others, but by himself. Have I created something satisfying to me?

"If to the person it has the "feel" of being "me in action," of being an actualization of potentialities in himself which heretofore have not existed and are now emerging into existence, then it is satisfying and creative, and no outside evaluation can change that fundamental fact."

And here we are, back to our locus of approval.

To combat our fear of expression we need to set ourselves as the source of judgement of our efforts, asking; "does this please me, represent me, feel like me?" If so, job done.

We particularly love that phrase, 'me in action'. Have I captured something of my unique me-ness in the expression of my creative output? Sod the judgement of the many-headed others, whom I can never satisfy in any totality.

Can I satisfy myself, at this stage I am at in the wider creative process, which will last my whole life?

If yes, then it's Creativity 1, Fear 0.

GETTING TO KNOW YOU
We are not saying any of this is easy. Far from it. It all takes practice and experience.

The best way to learn the difference between these Gremlins is to pay attention to ourselves as we write.

Those pesky saboteurs know us inside out and they know exactly how to play us. And so, our job is to get to know ourselves, and them, equally well, so that the next time **Completion-Phobic Gremlin** pops up saying, "Oh, this isn't quite what we hoped is it? How about you quit and start afresh?" we can smile, pat its head and say, "Sorry buddy, I'm onto you now. There's power in finishing what I have started. It's a promise I made to myself and my creativity, and one that I'm not willing to break. So, I'm getting to the finish line with this project, imperfect as it is. And then we'll see what's what."

And so, just when you didn't think it was possible, you've done it! You have navigated the many Gremlins who have attempted to stop you in your tracks, and strengthened your relationship with your creative self. You have finished the first draft of your writing project. You are truly UNSTOPPABLE.

Congratulations.

Now you can enjoy the space that exists past the finish line: **THE GREMLIN-FREE ZONE**, also known as flow.

CHAPTER SEVEN QUICK MAP

- After making progress you may have the urge to start a new project

- This can be down to fear of exposure, failure and judgement

- You can change your unrealistic expectations of both yourself and your work

- Learning to meet your own expectations is key to completing your creative journey

- There is power in finishing something

HOW AUTHORS BECOME UNSTOPPABLE #7
Emma Jane Unsworth, author of Animals (Cannongate)

There is a point I reach regularly, which I am sure all novelists reach regularly, around about Chapter 12, when I realise the perfect idea I had is becoming a shambolic, shameful reality. It always hurts. Because you always think you've got the perfect book until that point. But then you have to remember you can never have such a thing as the perfect book, because the act of creation involves translating an abstract into a form – and you are only human, and this is only the real world. So all perfect ideas will become imperfect realities in the end, if they are to become anything. You can always just leave them hanging in the ideas ether, of course, but these things tend to nag.

How do I get over this? I walk, I run, I drink wine, I talk to friends, I watch good movies, I watch dreadful TV, and sooner or later, I find I can push through in teeny, tiny increments, that difficult middle part until you get to the very end and it's downhill again. I also find it helpful to break the job down into sections. Turning points, if you like. When a character goes off in another direction, physically or mentally or both. Making it to the next turning point becomes like the next tree or lamp-post you've got to run to in a marathon, when the thought of the overall marathon is too much to take. Because the most important thing you can do – to truly know whether your idea is worth anything – is to get to the end of the first draft. Do whatever it takes to do that. Remember you can redraft, and redraft, and redraft – so it doesn't even have to be a great first draft, and probably won't be.

I keep five or six of my all-time favourite books to hand when I'm writing and when I need to, I just open one randomly and try and be inspired by the style. I also think, this only exists because someone finished it – so get on with it! That thing you're afraid of – of not being good enough – is nowhere near as bad as never having really tried.

CHAPTER 8

The Gremlin-Free Zone

Congratulations, you made it!

APPRECIATING YOUR CREATIVE JOURNEY

Well done for making it both to the end of this creative journey and the end of this book! We know it hasn't been easy. Wrestling with these Gremlins is tough. It might even seem to the uninitiated that creativity is nothing *but* problems…

But that's very far from the case.

The reason we've confronted you with Seven Gremlins rather than 'Seven Steps to Find your Creativity' is because we believe you don't actually *need* to find your creativity. Your creativity, like your heartbeat and your breath, is already yours to own. The bulk of your work is in rejecting all the Gremlins who would like you to believe otherwise.

YOU GOT PAST THE GREMLINS!

If you've managed to circumvent these beasts for long enough to complete a first draft, does that mean you are now free of the Gremlins forever?

HA! Nope.

A creative life means that these little fellas are always going to be along for the ride.

When you get ready to start your next project, so will they. They're as committed to protecting you as you are to realising your creative potential. And that's fine. These creative lessons are not something we learn once and then, BOOM! we've nailed it. Creativity is a life-long learning experience. We'll go off track and then correct our course, time and time again. But it doesn't matter. Creativity is always there waiting for us to return.

Eventually, when you get familiar enough with the Gremlins to ignore their wiles for a moment, you'll experience a blissful period when all the critical voices recede and there's just you and your work. When time stands still and you are utterly in the moment. You feel as though you are connected to something greater; plugged in, somehow, to a deeper source of creativity than your own self.

This is flow.

Flow state might last for minutes or hours. It might even last for days or weeks if you are incredibly lucky. Or it might only last for a few seconds. And it doesn't matter. Because all it takes is one momentary experience of this incomparable state to understand exactly why human beings so long to create. To understand that, when we connect with that flow of creativity, it seems to set light to some hidden magical spark inside us, making incredible transformations possible.

We're not talking about publishing deals or awards or wild success (though these things may well occur as a by-product, because this magic will be evident in your work).

We're talking about how creating can make us feel more whole, happier and more like our authentic selves.

The more you write, the more you'll discover that the lessons and wisdom gained from overcoming the challenges in completing a project can be applied to the rest of your life. And in the same way, what you learn in your life as you develop and grow as a person can be applied to your writing process.

This is the incredible secret of creativity: it doesn't just give us joy, or help us entertain, comfort and touch the lives of others.

It teaches us how to live.

And what could be a more worthwhile journey than that?

REFERENCES

i *The War of Art: Break Through the Blocks & Win Your Inner Creative Battles.*
Steven Pressfield, Black Irish Entertainment LLC. 2012.

ii Elizabeth Gilbert's 'Big Magic' podcast:
elizabethgilbert.com/magic-lessons

iii Amy Cuddy:
ted.com/talks/amy_cuddy_your_body_language_shapes_who_you_are

iv Tim Urban: waitbutwhy.com

v *Your Brain At Work, Strategies for Overcoming Distraction, Regaining Focus, and Working Smarter All Day Long.*
David Rock, Harper Business. 2009.

vi *Bird by Bird: Instructions on Writing and Life*
Anne Lamott, Bantam Doubleday Dell Publishing Group. 1980.

vii *Games People Play: The Psychology of Human Relationships*
Eric Berne, Penguin Life. 2016 (First published, 1964)

viii *Seducing the Demon: Writing For My Life*
Erica Jong, Tarcherperigee. 2007.

ix *A Guide to Rational Living*
Albert Ellis, Wlishire Book Company. 1975.

x Manoush Zomorodi:
ted.com/talks/manoush_zomorodi_how_boredom_can_lead_to_your_most_brilliant_ideas?

xi *An Experiment in Leisure*
Marion Milner, Routledge. 2011 (First published, 1937)

xii *What I Talk About When I Talk About Running*
Haruki Murakami, Vintage. 2009.

xiii *Big Magic: Creative Living Beyond Fear,* Elizabeth Gilbert, Bloomsbury Publishing, 2015.

xiv *Toward a Theory of Creativity.*
Carl Rogers, A Review of General Semantics. 1954.

END NOTES

WHAT NEXT ON YOUR CREATIVE JOURNEY?

We've loved going on this creative journey with you – thanks for having us along for the ride. We hope you've found some useful hints and tips, and have started to identify which of the Gremlins are most likely to pop up as your creative ventures pick up steam. Whatever they have in store – you're ready for them!

SO, WHAT NEXT?

At the beginning of this book we suggested that it would be useful for you to work on a writing project in parallel to reading *Seven Creative Gremlins*.

Did you manage to start? Or is still on your To Do list?

Whether you're deep into your project or teetering on the verge of beginning, now could be a good time to do some free writing to sharpen your insights into what you love about writing as well as identifying who and what hijacks your creativity.

How to use these prompts

We suggest picking one prompt at a time to use as part of your daily free writing practice. Set a timer for five minutes. Start with the prompt and see where it takes you.

Keep your hand moving, don't cross out, and don't worry about spelling, punctuation or grammar. If you get stuck, just keep returning to the prompt.

Remember, what you write doesn't have to make any sense; there is no way to get it wrong.

- "I write because…"
  (Why bother? What is the hook that entices me to write?)
- "The best thing about my writing is…"
  (What is the most encouraging thing I can tell myself about my writing?)
- "I don't write because…"
  (What are my top three reasons for never getting down to writing?)
- "My favourite thing about writing is…"
  (What have I most enjoyed about my writing project to date?)
- "I didn't expect to love…"
  (What has been the biggest surprise for me about getting stuck into writing?)
- "I didn't realise I…"
  (What have I discovered about myself that I didn't previously know?)
- "My future self wants me to know…"
  (What does 'me in the future' want to tell 'current me'?)

WANT MORE?

We've created a fantastic workbook, packed with tips and exercises to help you develop a positive mindset and exercises to supercharge your writing practice.

If you'd like to receive a FREE copy of your *Seven Creative Gremlins* workbook, go to: theunstoppableauthor.com/scgworkbook

EVEN MORE?

If you'd like further support, advice or inspiration, then come on over to theunstoppableauthor.com where we post regular articles, insights, author stories etc.

RECOMMENDED READING
The Artist's Way, Julia Cameron

Life and How To Survive It, John Cleese and Robin Skynner

Big Magic: Creative Living Beyond Fear, Elizabeth Gilbert

On Writing, Stephen King

Bird by Bird, Anne Lamott

An Experiment in Leisure, Marion Milner

On Becoming A Person, Carl Rogers

The Well of Being, Jean-Pierre Weill

ACKNOWLEDGEMENTS

We are immensely grateful to the many people who have played a part in transforming our idea into the finished book you now have in your hands.

Huge thanks to the following creatives who spent time with us discussing their creative journeys. We learned so much about the ebb and flow of creativity from their generous and candid conversations: Joe Banton, Martin Brew, Rhiannon Hodgeon, Brian King and Margit van der Zwan. And for her wisdom and guidance, Elaine Swords.

Thank you to all the authors who were willing to share an insight into their own struggles with Gremlins: Pippa James, Zoe Lambert, Andrea Mara, Maria Roberts, Sarah Tierney and Emma Jane Unsworth.

The following readers gave their time and offered invaluable feedback as part of the book's development. Thank you for your insights: Nick Brown, Sam Chambers, Olivia D'Silva, Jenny Hacker and Dawn Reeve.

We are grateful for the support of the following in all matters design and editorial: Sara Jaspan, Rhian McKay, Greg Thorpe.

And thanks for the fantastic cover design by Liam Relph.

We are so grateful to Mary and Terry Wilson for helping us to realise our project and bring it to life in the way our hearts desired. Thank you, thank you, thank you.

Nicola thanks Nick Brown for his support, his sanity, and for letting her test out her creative writing exercises on him – that he went on to write a cracking first novel just to prove they work was a nice twist.

Teresa will never tire of thanking Debs Gatenby for her unquestioning support, ideas and guidance. Your creativity inspired so much of this book and your creativity inspires me daily.

MEET THE AUTHORS
Nicola Jackson

I always knew I wanted to be a novelist but still it took me until age thirty to even make a start. First I became a bookseller, then a copywriter, journalist, editor, book reviewer, *girlfriend* of a writer (not, one should point out, an actual profession); circling my creativity over and over until finally I had to accept that I clearly wanted to write fiction myself, and had better bloody well get on with it. One up-tempo-typing-through-the-night montage later and my debut *The Gods of Love*, written as Nicola Mostyn, was published the year I turned forty. It was, and remains, a dream come true. But I was aware that what came up *while* I was writing the novel – the doubts, the fears, the horror of rejection – was the stuff of pure self-development. This became the subject of many conversations between me and my friend Teresa, who just happens to be an amazingly gifted Creativity Coach, and we decided to collaborate. We wanted to delve deeper into a side of writing that isn't always talked about: the psychological and practical blocks that face many aspiring writers but which, if anticipated, can help strengthen our relationship with creativity and make our lives truly magical.

Teresa Wilson

My earliest memory is of standing in front of an easel at nursery school, in my pinny, paintbrush in hand. I must have been about three. And I remember viscerally the fear of being presented with a blank sheet of paper and thinking, "I can't do it. I don't know what to do." Lord knows where that precociously early self-doubt came from, but I like to think I'm a trailblazer. I experienced young what many of us come to encounter in our lives; a point where playful, joyous, spontaneous creativity becomes plagued by thoughts of comparison, self-doubt and insecurity. Fast-forward 40+ years and I find myself working as a Creativity Coach, helping people work out how to get out of their own way when it comes to realising their potential. I continue to be terrified of easels and in deep awe of those who aren't afraid to put their creativity out there. One of those people is my great friend Nicola, and this book is the culmination of 20 years of conversations over coffee about what it means to grow – through discomfort, fuck-ups and fear – into our most authentic selves.

Printed in Great Britain
by Amazon

60562461R10092